I REMEMBER

Been There. Did That.

by Eugene Williams *Eugene W. 2013*

Sketch by Justin Williams

I REMEMBER THE GREAT DEPRESSION

ISBN #--978-0-615-37964-7

Printed in USA by:
Graphic Design, Inc.

I DEDICATE THIS BOOK

To my Mother and Dad who brought me into this wild world in hard times during the First Great Depression.

I dedicate this book to our troops, wherever they may be. Hopefully the government will buy a book for every soldier for his or her reading pleasure.

I thank the following people who have helped make this book
possible:

My wife Ann
Dan and Wilma Gulstad
John Hahn Jr.
Dorothy Rivard

TABLE OF CONTENTS

PART 1: THE HARD TIMES and THE WAR

CHAPTER 1 — Way back before the Roaring 20's

CHAPTER 2 — The 1930's — The Dust Bowl

CHAPTER 3 — The 1940's

CHAPTER 4 — Bottineau Grandma and Grandpa too

CHAPTER 5 — Back on the Farm

CHAPTER 6 — The Old Log House

CHAPTER 7 — Christmas on the farm

CHAPTER 8 — Tough Times

CHAPTER 9 — The Big War

CHAPTER 10 — The Big City

CHAPTER 11 — The good ole' 50's

CHAPTER 12 — After high school

CHAPTER 13 — Eagle Bend 1950's - 1960's

CHAPTER 14 — Jackson and the town that was

CHAPTER 15 — Bertha 1950's - 1960's

CHAPTER 16 — The Recession 1970's - 1980's

PART 2: SOME PEOPLE'S KIDS DID THE CRAZIEST THINGS

CHAPTER 17 — Things got better just like Ma said

CHAPTER 18 — Crazy things happening

CHAPTER 19 — Korea and the War

CHAPTER 20 — Chicken bones and buffets

CHAPTER 21 — Jack of all trades & meat packing buddies

CHAPTER 22 — More precious moments

CHAPTER 23 — Weiner dog

CHAPTER 24 — Cars and toys in my life

CHAPTER 25 — A Taiwan Experience

CHAPTER 26 — My horse Trigger

CHAPTER 27 — HDTV

CHAPTER 28 — Gumbo, Booya, and Crawdads

CHAPTER 29 — Castle Burgers and more Buffets

CHAPTER 30 — North Dakota gumbo

CHAPTER 31 — How times have changed

CHAPTER 32 — Dads and Moms do cry

CHAPTER 33—Krabby Kraft Car Parts

CHAPTER 34 — Uncle Sam calling

CHAPTER 35 — Eat noodle soup with chop sticks

CHAPTER 36 — Back home

CHAPTER 37 — The middle-age spread

CHAPTER 38 — Retirement time

CHAPTER 39 — Remember when

CHAPTER 40 — It's like this

CHAPTER 41 — More thoughts of the day

CHAPTER 42 — Real Estate

CHAPTER 43 — The Minnesota nut test

CHAPTER 44 — The order of the day

CHAPTER 45 — Saturday nights on the farm

CHAPTER 46 — Beer in the diaper bag

CHAPTER 47 — Quips and Quotes

CHAPTER 48 — Things got better again

CHAPTER 49 — These Golden Years

CHAPTER 50 — Does History repeat itself?

ABOUT THE AUTHOR

I am no real important person or anybody like that. I was born in the town of Bottineau, in that God forsaken state of North Dakota and raised in the Upper Midwest, Minnesota. Sometimes we are called the Upper Great Plains people.

I have pretty much been the runt of the family. My inseam is 28 inches. That's up the right leg on a good day. I like my pant legs above my ankles and the crotch up to my crotch. If my waist was 28 inches it would be much easier to buy pants. I have a dimple on my chin and a wart on my face. I think I inherited them from Norway Grandma. She had a wart on her face too.

I don't like the cold snowy weather anymore so guess I wouldn't make a good Eskimo.

I like antiques. I've been called an antique myself. My favorite fishing hat has some words on it that read "Antique Person, Highly Polished." The hat has a fly fishing lure on it just waiting to be casted into the water behind my house. I got that lure from a colleague, a friend from England who was also in the inspection trade. He didn't have time to go fishin' either. But he had a real racket going on. I can't tell more than that. If I did I'd be giving away his trade secrets.

Antiques, auctions, old cars, old toys, Chinese food and looking at women are my priorities in life but not necessarily in that order. My better half said more than once "quit looking at those girls". I simply responded to her "the day when I quit looking is when you better start worrying". That'l learn'er.

I've been seen coming and going to an auction with antique furniture and stuff piled on top of my little red truck like the Beverly Hills family heading west. I've lost more old stuff off the top of that truck than Carter has pills.

I've had some fun times. I've had some bad times. I've been places I loved and been places I do not want to talk about but I made the best of them all.

I am a picker and so is a buddy of mine but I am a picker of antiques.

INTRODUCTION

As I sat down to write this book I was amazed of the memories that came back to me from my childhood. Some of those memories were good and some were not so good. But it brings back a little humor and some of the daring and unusual true-life experiences when I was 3 years old during the First Great Depression up until the present time.

The lard and sugar sandwiches for school lunch tasted very good when we had nothing else. I thank you for your delicious home-made bread to make those sandwiches, Ma. Thank you for the hard work on the farm and railroad section gang, Dad. You put the food on the table for us kids or as they say here in Minnesota "you brought home the bacon".

My greatest wish is that Ma and Dad were here today so I could hear them laugh again when "some people's kids do the craziest things". I was one of those kids.

In a Twin City suburb there were 3 old dilapidated 2 story houses in a row, side by side that had a very personal touch in our history. The little town's people had names for them. They called them Faith, Hope & Charity. Every time we drove by them we called them by name.

And now--I have Faith, I have faith that this book will sell. I have Hope, I hope that this book will sell. I may need Charity if it doesn't sell. If nobody buys this book I may need to have a meeting and ask for a government bailout.

There is no real rhyme or rhythm here— the subjects jump around like an old tom cat on a hot tin roof but it is all true stuff as I remember it. Yes I know-- that's kind'a scary.

I spent many nights thinking of a name for this book. I want it to reflect some of my true experiences and to bring a little humor into your life. I've heard tell that if a person counts spokes in a chair or tile joints in a floor he might be on something or a little off his rocker? Well the only thing I was on was coffee. 1- - 2- - - 3- - -4- -

The names in this book are fictitious to protect the guilty. The pictures, the sketches and the words are mine and are authentic and real. They do not intend to harm or make fun of anyone but to the contrary.

If you like good, clean humor, dry or wet humor, you just gotta' read this book!! I hope it will make you laugh and enlighten your day at least a little bit.

More than once I've said to myself,-------- "self, I could write a book about that".

Well, here is that book.

I REMEMBER THE GREAT DEPRESSION
(That's kinda' Scary)

PART 1- The Hard Times and the War

PART 2- Better Times Came like Ma said they would

And Some Peoples Kids Did The Craziest Things

AND NOW

PART 1

THE HARD TIMES AND THE WAR

CHAPTER 1

WAY BACK BEFORE THE ROURING 20'S

My grandpa on Dad's side had come from England way back a long time ago around the late 1800's. Grandma on Dad's side came from Norway, Mundahl or Mondale town to be more accurate. (I don't think I'm any relation to Walter). Grandma on Ma's side fled from Czechoslovakia when times were tough there. Grandpa on Ma's side came from Germany. Anyway the grandmas and grandpas got together and did their thing and that's where I came from.

Norway Grandma, Dad, and Uncle C by grandma's first house on her 40 acre Homestead south of Eagle Bend, Minn., where eagles sore.

When I was little Dad told me that this old house burned down in about 1914. They built another house to replace it that is still in the family and still standing tall today.

Dad had told me about the 1929 Stock Market crash. He didn't play the stock markets but recalls the market soured in the 1920's due to easy credit and extensive corruption. There was a stock market bubble and everybody loved it. No one imagined anything would go wrong or no one saw it coming but on October 29, 1929 the Market Crashed. A Great Depression followed. Credit was frozen. Thousands and thousands of people lost their jobs. Approximately 14 million people were out of work in 1932 in the Great Plains area alone. Unemployment rose to 25%. There was no such help as unemployment compensation or Medicare. People couldn't borrow money. Taxes were raised. Approximately 5000 banks went broke by 1932. The suicide rate had soured to an all-time high. And production of the 1929 Indian $5 Gold piece was halted.

Some called these years "the roaring 20's. I guess the people in the bars danced and roared and danced and roared to the wee hours of the morning either to relieve their frustration or because they didn't have a way to get home. I think the thing that roared the most was Norway Grandma's old Flossy horse and the neighbors. The neighbors roared when Dad and Uncle Carl played at local barn dances to the tunes "The Irish Washer Women" and the "Orange Blossom Special" on the fiddle and the banjo. Barn dances were popular then. It helped take people's minds off of troubles and off of the economy.

**Dad and Uncle Carl playing at a local barn dance.
Dad on the fiddle, Uncle Carl on the banjo**

CHAPTER 2

THE 1930's—THE DUST BOWL

And then came a drought. Very little rain fell for several years. Only 10 inches of rain fell in the midwest in 1934. The heavy soil dried up and cracked. The sandy soil blew away like dust. And then came the Black Blizzard, the Dust Bowl from Texas, to Oklahoma, to Colorado and to Kansas. The wind took all the good top soil and blew it eastward across the country. Hundreds and hundreds of people died from the sand-lung disease. Mounds of dust were found 6 feet deep in the Texas panhandle. The biggest dust storm noted was black dust a mile high in the sky on April 14, 1935 and 850 million tons of the best part of Texas, Oklahoma, Colorado and Kansas was blown east into the Atlantic Ocean. Later when I was three years old Dad told me they called that day "Black Sunday".

Then came the spiders. They multiplied like rabbits and ate the crops. Then came the centipedes. They multiplied like rabbits and ate the crops. Then came the grasshoppers. They multiplied like rabbits and ate the crops. Then came the jack rabbits. They multiplied like rabbits do and they ate the crops that were left.

About the only thing left were some tumble weeds. People ate tumble weeds cause there wasn't anything else left after the spiders, the centipedes, the grasshoppers and jack rabbits ate everything else.

Static electricity caused by the sand being blown against metal farm machinery shocked people when they touch it.

Some sand and dust came as far north as Minnesota. Ma hung wet feed sacks over the house windows and doors to help catch some of the dust that came through the cracks around the windows and the walls. Dad hung an old piece of scrap binder canvas over the top of the chimney outside to keep dust out that was coming down into the stove.

People were asking the government for rain makers. One old guy in a nearby town claimed he could make rain. He asked for donations and more donations for his secret method and fancy equipment but his system didn't produce any rain. Thus came the term "the rain maker".

Many people packed up some of their most important belongings and headed to California where things were supposed to be better. Their travel to the west was overbearing with extreme heat in the summer and extreme cold in the winter. The cars broke down in the mountains. Tires went flat from the hard rocky mountain roads. No tires were available along the way. No parts were available to repair them. They barely had enough food along to keep them going until they reached California. When they did reach their destination food was expensive and scarce there too. Gas, tires and sugar was rationed nationwide. There wasn't enough work and housing for all who went there. Many had to live in tent cities and scrounge or beg for food. Well as you may know, the tent cities didn't have any running water and no plumbing and no electricity. They had to haul drinking water and try to live off the land.

The drought finally ended in 1939. The Dust Bowl ended about the same time. But the effects of that First Great Depression had not ended.

Some say that Roosevelt's New Deal and World War II was the best thing that happened cause it brought back jobs and it brought back the economy. I believe that was politically correct but I am not touching politics with a ten foot pole.

CHAPTER 3

THE 1940's

Anyway, time went on and I remember Norway Grandma putting on a pair of her darn yarned homemade socks and wore them until they had holes in the bottom so big that they slipped up above her ankle and up her leg. Then she would re-yarn the darn socks at the toes and heels. She yarned them socks until the socks got so thick she couldn't hardly get her shoes on. In those days they had what was called yarn balls where they pulled the sock over the ball to shape it before mending or yarning. I called them "darn yarn sock balls" and they were made of wood cause it was the most affordable product. Grandma didn't have electricity so she didn't have any light bulbs which worked real good for darn sock yarning.

I saw Grandma get out of bed one morning with her socks still on her feet. They kept her feet warm in bed and out of bed until she limped over to the wood burning stove in the living room or sometimes by the wood burning cast iron kitchen stove. You see Uncle C was staying with Grandma on the homestead 40 and he was the master wood cutter, wood chopper, wood hauler, and the wood stove fire tender, the hunter, the trapper, the cow milker, the egg picker. I guess Dad took care of old "flossy" horse and did the field work, all 13 acres.

Dad told me all these true stories about when he and Uncle C took turns going to school cause they had to milk the cows, feed the chickens, pick the eggs, care for and harness the horses, farm the 13 acre field, and take care of Grandma to keep her strong. And she was strong, she was old but she was strong. She kept strong after England Grandpa W. left her. Dad never really knew his Dad and was 4 years old when his Dad passed away.

Norway Grandma didn't have a lot but she had strength and she had that little old house, a small shack barn for old "Flossy" horse. I vaguely remember old Flossy when I was 3 or 4 years old. Flossy was Dad's and Uncle C's tractor. They didn't have to buy gas for her. She had plenty gas of her own (we won't get into that any farther).

Uncle C (Uncle Carl) and Old Flossy Horse

Norway Grandma always made home-made bread from scratch. Sometimes she scratched her head and sometimes she scratched something else when she discovered she didn't have any yeast, which was put in the dough to make it raise. Dad always ate the "heel" of the bread. I think it was because he didn't want to see it go to waste. We were told that no food would be wasted. It was too expensive to be given to the hogs or chickens.

One day Dad's Uncle Chris came over and told Dad he had located a 40 acre piece of land that Dad may be interested in buying. Anyway one rainy day Dad, Uncle Chris, one of my brothers and me climbed into the old car that I think was a modern "T" Ford? Yah, that's what it was, a modern "T" Ford as I called it then, and drove over to take a look at the 40 in the woods about seven miles away. The road over to this 40 was no more than a narrow cart trail full of ruts with buck brush growing up to the edge. There was no shoulder on the road. There was no ditch alongside the road so water ran on the road as much as off the road. I remember it was raining pitchforks and hammer handles all that day.

Anyway later on Dad bought that 40 acre woods and buck brush and cleared out a spot about 100 feet square about 200 feet off of the road to move the one room house onto. I don't know what Dad bought the land with, it must have been his good looks or I'm thinking Uncle Christ may have sold a couple horses and helped Dad buy that 40.

Ma and Dad's first house on Grandma's homestead 40.

Dad and Ma built their first house out by the chicken coup on Grandma's 40. This was the one room house with a sheet hung across the middle to make a 2 room house. One day Dad said "we going to move this house". Those words didn't agree with me so I crawled under the kitchen table and hid cause I didn't want to move the house. I was 4 years old and just didn't want to move anything.

Now you gotta' hear this---Dad went down to the swamp on the homestead 40 where we had been living in this 2 room shack (a 1 room divided by a curtain across the middle, that made 2 rooms) by Grandma and cut a couple big pine trees and placed them under that 2 room shack for skids.

Dad knew the local road grader man so he got him to hook on and skid that house on the road for 7 miles to the new 40 in the boondocks three and a half miles north of town. The tree skids were worn down halfway when we got there. I was so mad at the road grader man too cause he ran over my favorite plum tree and ruined all the plums before he got the house out onto the road. I guess their priorities were different than mine.

Dad used those 2 worn down timbers for the foundation of the first barn that he built in the fall of 1941 just before the big storm and blizzard came. What a barn, it was wood all right except for the roof which was wide blade swamp grass that was supposed to shed the rain. Dad had lot of wide blade swamp grass cause about half of the 40 acres was swamp. Well after a year or so it didn't shed much rain. It seemed dryer outside than inside so we milked the cows outside in the rain for a while.

Some time in the mid 40's Norway Grandma was getting old and decripilated so Dad had her come to stay with us on the farm. Grandma didn't have many teeth left and those that she did have were getting bad. Her eye site was real bad too. She told us about things she remembered as a kid like coming across the big pond from Norway when she was 8 years old with not much more than the clothes on her back.

I remember she picked up my little sister one time because she was crying. Grandma had sister's feet up in the air and her head hanging down. But she was Grandma, my Grandma. And I remember the night Grandma had passed away in our house and they carried her out during the middle of the night in a big basket. The next morning Dad told us kids that Grandma had died.

I cannot forget that I would walk to school and back 1 ½ miles each way when in the 1st grade when it was 40 degrees below zero (that is – 40 F.) in 4 feet of snow. The road seemed like it was up hill both ways.

The teacher had a bench up on top of the big round wood stove where we would sit there to keep warm. There were only 20 kids in the whole school, grades 1 thru 8. I was lucky because usually only 5 or 6 kids came so we could all sit above the stove until noon, at least. The picture below is of the country grade school I went to for grades 1-5. *And yes, there was no indoor plumbing there either!!* That is me in the bibbed overalls with the hair parted down the middle.

Crider School-District 98
on the east road 2 miles north of E B dump

The local farmer had a goat fenced in about 20 feet from the school house. Us kids teased that goat until he or maybe she rammed through the fence and followed us right into the school house. Oh, it was a he cause it had horns. Anyway he did a big mess on the floor and then jumped up on the teacher's desk and did a mess on it. Boy, what a mess! The teacher gave us real hell for that. She had no sense of humor. I thought it was fun. Mrs. teacher said " we got to have classes outside for a couple days until the gagging smell goes away".

Dad worked on the railroad section gang to support us kids and Ma. That was a back-breaker job if there ever was one.

The railroad section gang

In about 1948 the electric company determined they needed more income so they ran electricity by our place even though we were the only farm on that one mile stretch of gravel road.

Dad never finished the 3rd grade in school but he had the smarts and figured it all out and installed electric into the house and barn on the farm. He put three lights in the house and a couple in the barn. That's the barn that had the grass roof? The roof had rotted away and gone buy-buy by now and it was almost livable in there for cattle now. You see Dad put a real wood roof on the barn to replace the wide blade swamp grass roof. When I say almost livable I mean that we didn't have any gutters in the barn floor yet so their waste kind'a went all over the place.

We didn't have indoor plumbing in the house yet, either. Oh boy, those winters were cold out there in that outhouse.

He improved the cow milking situation by putting in a vacuum milking machine system, a concrete floor in the barn and yes, gutters in the barn so now the cow fluids had a place to run instead of just flowing all over the floor. That was a very good move Dad. That milking machine sure beat the old way of yanking those things and squeezing them nearly to death to get the milk out.

Now with electricity on the farm and a furnace in the basement of the house with a blower, things were beginning to look up. I know heat rises but without a good furnace there wasn't much heat upstairs.

You see, by now Dad had put an addition on the house. He made a room that would later be a bathroom. He made a bedroom downstairs on the main floor and he made an upstairs room for us kids to sleep in. Then down came that bed sheet curtain divider that had been making that 1 room house into a 2 room house. Miracles had never seized to amaze me. It was still cold upstairs in the winter. I remember more than one morning us kids woke up with frost on the walls by the bed but we got used to that. Most of the time I just pulled the quilt over my head so my breath would warm me up pretty good. Sometimes we slept with our cloths on to keep warm. My brother had it figured out – he put his overalls under the covers to keep them warm. Insulation cost money so there wasn't any insulation in the upstairs ceiling. We just piled more quilts on the bed. Ma made quilts so that was no problem. We could have done like Bottineau Grandpa did—he pasted newspapers on the ceiling of his log house for insulation. Of course the paste was made with flour and water so it wasn't too expensive but Ma always said "things will get better some day".

Things did get a little better so Dad got the local water well digger to drill a modern well right by the house. We really had the world by the tail now. That 16 foot deep hand dug well down by the barn was petering out anyway. (That was the one that old Andrew witched it in and said we would hit water 16 feet down but we had to go 16 feet and 4 inches?) We finally got running water into the kitchen first. Then Dad made that bathroom inside the house. Well it was about time cause the old outhouse was getting dilapidated and infiltrated and stinky and it was full again and needed to be moved again and that kind of stuff, if you know what I mean. If you have been there, you know what I mean. I've been there. I Did that. I remember.

The door had fallen half way off the outhouse and Ma said to Dad "you got'a do something with that door out there". So Dad moved the outhouse into the woods, dug a hole, put the little house over the hole and turned it around facing the other direction.

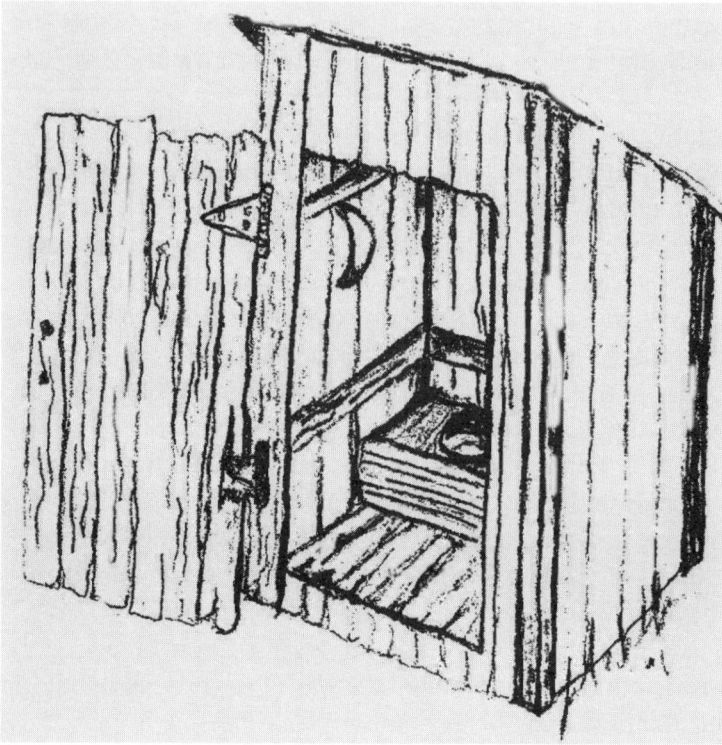

This sketch by Justin Williams

As time went on Dad put a toilet in the bathroom inside the house? Yah, inside the house. Now we did have the world by the tail, especially in the winter time. And a bathtub—that sure was nice too.

And then there was the neighbor kid who helped us try to sell watermelons. Freddie D was his name. He lived across the road from the old Crider Schoolhouse. Freddie lived with his sister and his Dad (old man as he called him). Freddie and his old man were excellent hunters and the best sharp shooters if there ever was one. They lived in a 2 room shack made of wood with 4x8 sheets of particle board nailed up for the ceiling. Half of the ceiling was ready to fall down cause Freddie would sit there and shoot the nails in the ceiling and drive them in until they disappeared. His Dad just laughed and said " I can do that too. See?" that's what they mean when they say "he's a chip off the old block". He was the best shooter ever seen, we would go hunting in the woods and Freddie says " I'll get that partridge in the tree." I would say "what partridge in what tree?" Freddie didn't have a shot gun like most people did cause he said they cost too much and the shells cost too much. So Freddie raised his 22 caliber rifle, fired one shot and down came a partridge with the neck shot off. Beyond me how he could even see that bird but to shoot the neck off, that was something. Freddie and his Dad had a couple riding horses too. He would come to our place sometimes in the dark a riding that horse not only without a saddle but without a bridle. It was pitch dark, so dark you couldn't see your hand in front of your face but he had that horse trained that way. He lost me in the dark one time cause I couldn't see hide nor hair of him or his horse. Freddie was part Native American and one of the best friends I had. He was one great guy. He smoked cigarettes like a chimney. He thought he smoked a lot if he had 4 cigs by noon. Heck, when I smoked I would have sucked down 4 cigarettes before I got out of bed. Kids, Don't Try That At Home.

CHAPTER 4

BOTTINEAU GRANDMA—GRANDPA TOO

Grandma and Grandpa did their thing and settled in the Turtle Mountains near Bottineau, Nord-da-koda in about the early 1920's. According to the local historians' "show and tell", Bottineau had been founded in 1884 and was growing by leaps and bounds by 1890's.

BIRD'S-EYE VIEW OF BOTTINEAU, N. D.

Bottineau in 1897

In the mid 1940's the economy temporarily got a little better for us on the farm. Every so often we would take a trip up to Bottineau Grandma's and Grandpa's. I remember the old car Dad had. I think it was a '29 Chevy, if my memory serves me right. Oh boy, that's kinda' scary. The Chevy wasn't bad on gas, probably 15 MPG. Gas was 15-20 cents a gallon. The Chevy was real bad on oil consumption. That Chevy burned so much oil that Dad would stock up on used drain oil from the local service station before we left for the trip. When we stopped for gas at the full service stations Dad would say "check the gas and fill'er up with oil". Well they filled the gas tank with gas but

Dad filled the engine with oil by just dumping in 3 or 4 quarts of used drain oil that Dad recovered from the local garage guy in town. I guess they called that "recycling". Dad knew how much oil he needed to dump in the motor by the oil pressure gauge reading. The service station attendant just laughed and giggled and threw up his hands.

That Chevy motor burned 10 quarts of oil on the 475 mile trip. Dad said to the attendant "Hey that ain't bad, I need to stop every 50 miles and scoop water out of the swamp and put in the radiator too". I don't know if they had anti-freeze yet and if there was Dad couldn't really afford it anyway.

Uncle M and Auntie L drove that trip to Bottineau too. He had a '29 Mopar Plymouth that burned 12 gallons of oil, yes gallons of oil on that same trip. Uncle M always got used drain oil from the local service station too. He took 3 or 4, 5 gallon cans along on that trip to Bottineau Grandma's in northern Nord-da-koda. I was there one time when they left to go there and that Mopar put so much smoke in the air it looked like a chimney. In today's standards he would probably be above the legal pollution limit and would get ticketed for over active environmental disobedience.

Anyway when we got to Bottineau Grandma's she always had homemade bread ready. I often wondered if she knew we were coming up or not cause of the fresh bread. I don't think Ma phoned Grandma cause we didn't have a phone. But Ma did write a letter sometimes to clue her in that the brats were coming to visit. That's where Ma got her smarts from. The smarts rubbed off real good, Ma. Grandma and Grandpa had an old wood burning stove too, just like everyone else up there in Nord-a-ko-da. They were only 15 miles from town but may as well been 1500 miles from town as far as having electricity.

Now Bottineau Grandpa, contrary to stories I've heard was far from lazy. Besides raising hay for the cattle and horses he made wooden boats and had a boat and bait rental business right in the front yard down the hill on the lake where they lived. That was Lake Metigoshi in the Turtle Mountains. He had about 8 boats down at the dock for rent. Well somebody's kids would come up there and visit and we all would grab a boat and take them out on the lake and stuff and when people came to rent a boat Grandpa had to holler out to us " bring in a some boats cause people want to go fishin". It was fun and Grandpa never really got real mad. At least he didn't show it. He was the best Grandpa.

Grandpa made a welding machine for his shop too. It was powered by an old John Deere tractor, a model D John Deere. The Deere had steel wheels originally and Grandpa converted it to rubber tires and stuff. He also made a homemade wood splitter machine. It had a big steel wheel about 10 feet in diameter with ax blades fastened around the circumference that split the wood as it rotated. Grandpa rigged up counter weights on it so a Briggs and Stratton engine powered it ok.

The cows were Grandma's problem. Grandpa said he wasn't about to yank those teats and that he had more important things to be doing. So Grandma and cousin Duffy milked the cows, 10 or 12, I guess, carry the milk to the house about 150 yards, separated the cream from the milk with the old dilapidated hand crank separator machine and then carry the skim milk back to the barn and feed it to the young calves. Now the cream that was separated out was used for coffee and to make homemade ice cream. And kids think they have it rough today? And remember Grandma's Maytag wash machine with a gasoline Maytag engine on it. That was modern for her when she got that. That engine was " temper mental". By that I mean--If it started, it started, if it wouldn't, well, it just wouldn't.

CHAPTER 5

BACK ON THE FARM

Even though sometimes we had only lard and sugar for our bread we did have real butter most of the time. Dad said "if we don't have anything else we are going to have butter". The local town creamery truck came around the country every day to pick up the milk which we had put in cans. We could leave a message on the milk can telling the hauler how many pounds of butter we wanted and he would leave that much butter. I remember the times when the butter used up most of the milk profit. The money transaction part was automatically taken care of at the creamery with trust. Trust? One thing we had in those days in a small town was trust. (Not to get off the subject but in those days we could trust people, neighbors helped neighbors, farmers helped farmers, businesses helped businesses.) We had a great neighbor who lived about ¾ mile across the swamp as the crow flies where we could stop to warm up on the way to school. The first time we met them, I was 4, Dad said "they are the Ellig's family. I couldn't say that name so I called them "Eggs". (Remember that Willie?)

And we didn't have to worry about drugs. Drugs were not around, oop-so, unknown about in our small town area where eagles soared.

Ma was a "chip off the old block", the Bottineau Grandma and Grandpa block. Ma made home-made bread too but she couldn't make it fast enough for her rug rats and Dad cause it was so good when it was warm that we all went crazy over it and gobbled it down like it was the last piece of food on earth. Ma put too much yeast in the dough one time. She went to town and when she got back the dough was raised too much. It was hanging over the edge of the pan, over the edge of the table and down to the floor. Somebody was supposed to watch the bread. I guess that somebody was me but instead of watching the bread I went out and played with the two-wheeled cart that us kids called the "thing cart" and with my Gene Autry™ gun and holster. Gene was my idol. 1----2-----3---. Anyway I heard some new words come out of Ma's mouth that day, some of them even she could hardly pronounce. Anyway Ma pulled up the sagging bread dough, pretended to squeeze off the part that touched the floor, put it in oven of the wood cook stove to bake it. "Ma, I saw you put that floored dough back in the pan, didn't you? But that's alright".

I loved Ma's bread so much that later on I asked her if she would bake bread for me after I got married. Guess what? Ma was getting worn out from years of laboring more than full time so I didn't win that one. Ma's home-made pies were good too as long as it was rhubarb, strawberry, pumpkin, squash, apple, cherry, berry, peach, pear, blueberry, mincemeat, raspberry, or anything similar. Ma used her thumb to make a neat pattern around the edge of the crust. I've heard that some people use their store-boughten' teeth to make a fancy design around the edge of the pie crust but that really takes the cake.

Our first water well was a hand-dug hole down in the swamp about $1/8^{th}$ mile from the house. The water was muddy, the cattle walked near there and drank from it too and stuff like that so the water was not real good tasting. We hauled water from the neighbors for a while until Dad hired an old water well witcher to witch where to dig a well. This was in early 1941. This may be the farthest thing for some to believe but if I wouldn't have seen it with my own eyes I wouldn't believe it either. Anyway let us call him Andrew. So Andrew went down into the muddy swamp, cut himself a willow branch that was fork shaped, like a "Y". He cut it nice and neat, to a length that suited him for his show which I thought was make-believe. He asked Dad approximately where he wanted the well to be. Dad said "well, lets put the well some place alongside the path between the house and the barn. That would be real good". So Andrew he starts walking up and down back and forth between the house and the barn while holding his green willow stick and curving it and twitching it around, up and down and all of a sudden the darn stick made a twitch and pointed down toward the ground and old Andrew has a heck of a time pulling it back up. Andrew said "right there, right there is water". It was right long side the path to the barn about 4 feet from the path. Dad said "well, how far down do we have to dig to get it". Andrew said "16 feet down you will hit water". Well nobody believed him including myself. A couple neighbors were there too cause they had heard about Andrew witching for water before but they had to see it happen. I started to laugh. Dad said "how can it be?" Andrew said again "16 feet to water if you dig right here, right here where my foot is".

So Dad finally believed him, after all Dad had asked him to do it. He got some neighbors around. They built a wooden frame, got a bucket and rope and some shovels and started digging about a 4 foot square hole. As time went on, somebody had to climb into the hole and fill up the bucket with the clay dirt. Digging was hard work. Stones didn't help the digging either. Dad built a wooden curb that slid down as the hole got deeper so it wouldn't cave in on the guy in the hole plus we would loose the well. I remember the guy in the hole one day got hit on the nose with the crank that was used to turn the drum and lift the bucket up and down. He had one heck of a bloody nose for a while. I remember that so well.

Anyway after 3 or 4 days of digging Dad was down in the hole and he said "I am down 16 feet and no water Andrew". Andrew wasn't digging, he was just supervising. Supervising I don't know what, but he was doing it. Andrew told Dad to dig down one more shovel depth. OK. So dad had to believe Andrew cause he was this far down and didn't want to start a different hole someplace else so he put the shovel down on the clay, put his big foot on the shovel and jabbed it down into the dirt. All of a sudden and I do mean sudden I heard Dad a whoopin' and a hollorin' "we got water, we got water". Dad looked up at us and smiled and I could see he was misty-eyed, as some call it. But he had tears in his eyes as big as horse turds. He was one happy camper that day. Old man Andrew just said, "I told you so". Now believe this story—it is true. I was there. I saw it. I remember I had tears in my eyes too, as big as little horse turds cause I was only a little boy.

As time went on I got to be 5 years old in the fall of 1941. The worst snow storm in the history of Minnesota came on Armistice Day November 11, 1941 and piled a snow drift 14 feet deep over the mail box out by the road. We were snowed in for a while but the horses and sled got us to town for necessary staples to survive on. Sometimes the horses almost got stuck in the snow. The local road grader man couldn't plow through the snow drift so they (maybe the county) came over with a caterpillar tractor and went cross wise over the road and gouged out some of the snow so the road grader man could get through with his plow. They worked at that 1 mile stretch of road about 3 days to get it open so a car could navigate through it. We really didn't have to go to town for a while. We were living off the land, off the farm, off the canned goods in the basement that Ma had canned during the previous summer (if there were any left after somebody's kids got into the basement and started eating them, quart by quart). Boy, that was good sauce as I remember.

CHAPTER 6

THE OLD LOG HOUSE

Great Uncle Chris Nuland's Log House

I remember this old log house when I was about 3 ½ years old. Uncle Chris, great uncle to me, and wife Johanna lived in this log house all their lives. There was one room downstairs (two if you want to count the pantry that was under the stairway). There was two rooms upstairs and there was a real wooden wall dividing them apart. There was no sheet hanging in this house to separate the rooms. They had real walls. To the best of my knowledge (that's kinda' scary) Chris and Johanna lived here all their lives.

Uncle Chris was a big Norwegian. He had a Norwegian mole on his face too. Johanna was a lovable little Norwegian lady who did the daily cooking on her cast iron stove in the kitchen living room. Chris took care of his little Johanna as if she was a cuppie doll. In the winter he split wood and carried enough into the house for the night and stacked it behind the stove.

Uncle Chris and one of his brothers Ole and his sister Jennie (my grandma) had come across the pond from Norway when Grandma was 8 years old. The story is that their name was Peterson in Norway and when they came here to what they called the New Land, they changed their name to Nuland because there were so many Petersons here already. They settled around Eagle Bend area where eagles sore. But Ole, he wanted to go further west and find some water so he could fish and trap so he struck out, probably on foot, and ended up on Lake Metigoshi, Bottineau County, Nord-a-koda. Ole homesteaded a place on the southwest bay of the lake.

Unfortunate things happened in those days (wives passed away, husbands passed away). There was no exception in our family as Ole's wife had passed away. There was no exception to the Hahn side of the family when a little old lady Dora's husband, L. Hahn had passed away. (who later became my Great Grandma Hahn), Now get a load of this—Uncle Ole got up the nerve and asked that little old lady Dora (my Great grandma Hahn to be) to marry him and they lived in a little log house on the big lake in the Turtle Mountains. Great Grandma Hahn wasn't my Great Grandma yet but one of her sons became my Grandpa Hahn when one of his daughters became my Ma. OH BOY!

Anyway Grandpa Hahn wasn't Grandpa yet until he hooked up with a lady that came across the pond from Czechoslovakia and they did their thing and Ma arrived into the world. Miracles never seize to amaze me. The lady from Czechoslovakia was my Bottineau Grandma from then on.
WOW! Now I understand the song "I'm my own Grandpa".

I remember my Norway Grandma, Jennie, telling that she came over with the cloths on her back and a few other things. She had a small oval box, a gold colored plow lapel pin and a sea shell. She gave each of us kids a trinket that she brought from Norway. Grandma gave me the large seashell and said that when you hold it up by the ear you can hear the sound of the ocean. That's what she always told me anyway. I got our kids believing it too. Hope our kids will pass it down to their little rug rats.

Uncle Chris was always busy like chopping wood and carrying it in the house and stuff. One evening he carried in much more wood than normal and stacked it beside the old cast iron stove. Johanna asked him why he was carrying in so much wood tonight. He told her that she would need it when he was gone. Chris slowly walked up the long steep stairs to his room as he did every day for an evening nap. He normally took a nap every day but this one was not normal. It was his last one. He's gone now.

CHAPTER 7

CHRISTMAS ON THE FARM

Some people's kids, yes me too, would walk up to the north 40, that was the 40 acres Dad bought that joined the first new 40 by the road with all the buck brush where Dad and Ma moved the 2 room house ? (You know? The one that Dad hired the road grader man to skid 7 miles down the road from Grandma's homestead 40)?

Buying a Christmas tree in town was not an option. Cutting down a pine tree for Christmas was the option. Some years there weren't any trees for sale in either local town I guess cause nobody could really afford a tree or there was not enough demand cause of the money situation.

Anyway us kids ran out of small trees on Dad's and Ma's farm so we thought about sneaking onto the neighbor's place and cut one but we scraped that idea cause the trees were very close to their house and we were brought up better than that. Of course I was told one time that it appeared I was born in the basement and never brought up. Anyway we had to climb a big full grown pine tree and cut the top off to make a Christmas tree. It worked but we finally ran out of big tree tops too. Then we had to settle for a branch from a big tree and man did they look funny? They were flat instead of round like a normal tree. Ma said "the tree is flat so we need to set it in a corner and put on a lot of bulbs and stuff so it will look somewhat like a tree". We had to tie it and nail it to the wall so it wouldn't fall over. We had the funniest tree around the whole neighborhood. We didn't care, it was our tree. We decorated it with those shinny icicle things and stuff. Sure glad it was green. That helped a little.

CHAPTER 8

TOUGH TIMES

Been there. Did that. I remember.

Back then the best joke around the neighborhood was " if you got lucky and won $100,000 what would you do with it?" The neighbor farmer simply replied with a dog-eaten' grin "I'll just keep farming until it's all gone".

Yeah farming was rough then. I'm not saying it is easy now cause it isn't. Dad couldn't afford a regular silo so he used snow fencing to hold the silage and stacked it 3 or 4 tiers high. That snow fence had no insulation factor so the silage froze about 2 feet in from the edge. Dad had us kids help him chop that frozen silage so he could take down a tier of the fence as the silage was used up.

Meanwhile Ma always raised a lot of chickens on the farm. She had several hundred female chicken hens. I remember sometimes we had to wash 100 dozen eggs a day to take to town and sell. After a few years of that Ma chickened out. The farm wasn't large enough to raise grain for the chickens so Ma had to buy grain from the middle man store in town. That was as about as profitable as buying an army. We ate a lot of eggs too. We had fried eggs, poached eggs, scrambled eggs, boiled eggs, eggs scrambled into the fried spuds. I asked Ma once "Ma, how do you skin the eggs". When I think about that now I meant to say " Ma how do you skin the boiled eggs"?

Those were tough years for all the small farmers. They had a hard time making ends meet. They would delay paying Peter so they could pay Paul. Dad and Ma were in the small farmer category. Sometimes us kids only had lard and sugar sandwiches to take to school for lunch. We learned to eat left-overs, if there were any left after us kids pigged out. Lard was cheap. It was even cheap to buy if we didn't have any left from a hog we butchered. Butchering was sometimes a community thing. A neighbor or so would come and help take turns sliding the dead hog up and down in the scolding barrel of water to soften the hair and stuff. Sugar was rationed but it was necessary for survival. The best food we had was Ma's homemade baked bread.

Yes those were hard times but I consider myself fortunate for not having to live in my car as some people had to cause they had no choice.

Ma said "we gotta' have a garden, everybody has a garden, you know. I want you kids to help. We need to grow some cucumbers so I can make some pickles. We need to grow about 1 or 2 acres and if that is more than we need for pickles you kids can take the extras to town and sell them but you got to pick them everyday before they get too big". "The little cukes bring the most money". We called them cukes for short.

Ma knew what she doing. She had been around and wasn't born just yesterday. So we talked Dad into letting us grow 1 ½ acres of cukes. We had a weed digger on wheels and a hoe. Us kids wore out a lot of pants knees picking cucumbers to make pickles. That was our spending money.

We grew about an acre or acre and a half of cucumbers but (we called them pickles). We picked them every day to get the small ones cause they brought the most money. I bet that is why I have this crazy backache today. There was a pickle factory in Eagle Bend town and a market for our pickles. We would haul them in and watch them grade the cukes and get paid the same day. Then we would be on our way to the ice cream store to get somebody else's homemade ice cream.

Bro Les peddled the muddy country roads in rain selling Cloverleaf Ointment to get enough money to buy a Daisy air rifle and a Tom Mix ring. He wore out a couple tires and more than one pair of pedals. Sometimes Ma would ask "where's Les"? Cause sometimes he was gone from dusk till dawn a pedaling down the that muddy road to the neighbors in the country. Most people didn't have much money but it was good ointment and it was reasonable and they didn't have to go town to get it so Les made some sales. He sold a tin here and a tin there. Every little bit helped.

Us kids grew watermelons in the field behind the house too. We set up a watermelon stand out by the road and figured we would give people a good buy at 9 cents a pound. We even had a scale out there to weigh the melon in front of the customers cause we didn't want anybody to think we may be screwing them. I thought we would really make a lot of money cause the watermelons were really nice and ripe, very good tasting and we had a discounted price. Discounted compared to who? I guess we didn't figure that in our business. What we didn't think about was that we were the only farm on that mile of road that went between two other roads that really went nowhere and there was no traffic on the road except our next door stingy, tight neighbor. Watermelon sales--there were none. Anyway we didn't give up that easy.

Us kids were so persistent to make some money (I guess maybe that's the Scotch part of me) that we dug a bunch of skunks (I mean a real big bunch) out of the ground to sell the skins and hopefully make a ton of money. Those skunks had a hole down in the ground in the pasture on Norway grandma's homestead. We had to be careful so the skunks wouldn't spray juice on us. Yeah, we called it juice. Back in those days the real word for it was considered vulgar. (more than that was considered vulgar). Grandma wouldn't dare to wear shorts outside. It was even improper for a lady to expose her angles. You must believe that one.

Anyway we lit a little fire over the skunk hole in the ground and put some green grass on the fire so it made smoke. The smoke drove the buggers out another hole and we quickly grabbed them by the tail and hold them up in the air and then clobbered them with a big stick before they sprayed on us. HINT #1: Be sure you quickly hold them up by the tail or else!

We took them home to Dad and said "Dad, look what we got". Dad says "OH Boy!" Anyway we skinned them out, stretched the skins over a homemade wooden board thing and dried the skins and asked Dad if he would ship the hides some place to get some money for us kids. Dad knew what was up but he fell for it and said "ok but you need to make a strong wood box, you need to make it tough so it won't break during shipping". So we made it strong, so tough that it must have weighed 85 lbs. Dad said ok so us kids boxed them all up in that wood crate that we made from scrap 2x4 lumber we found around the barn yard (pee-uuu) and got them ready for shipping. I estimate today that the furs and box total weight was about 100 lbs. You know none of us kids knew that any box over 70 lbs would be special delivery and real pricey. We probably wouldn't care anyway cause we already had it in our mind to stick Dad with the shipping.

Anyway, Dad sent it off to the big city fur buying place by special truck delivery. One day we got a check for about $1.50 for the 25 furs we had sent. Dad knew they weren't worth a whole lot but didn't say anything. He was glad we were ambitious and wanted to learn something on our own. Dad got the raw deal cause we did stick it to him and he paid the shipping cost. Us kids figured That learned 'em cause he wouldn't let us take the car and go digging skunks again.

I remember when we were skinning those skunks Uncle Oscar stopped by on one of his walking trips on the way home to Duluth from North Dakota. He said "man them things stink bad and what you going to do with them"? We told him that we were going to make a lot of money.

Uncle Oscar (he was a Mundahl so I guess he was a half uncle) from way back and he had a brother Ben. Ben was a tall man, Oscar was small and short. They both stayed smart. They never got married but lived like hermits in the north woods of Minnesota. Uncle Oscar walked out to North Dakota every fall to pick potatoes in the potato fields. When the harvest was over he would walk down to our place and visit a couple days and continue back to his little shack in the north woods. They both knew how to rough it and they roughed it.

Roughing it was when :

You chew snoose instead of smoking cigarettes so the wind won't blow smoke in your eyes

You smoke corn silk instead of tobacco

You have lard and sugar sandwiches for school lunch

You have to walk to school cause gasoline was rationed and barely affordable cause it cost 20¢ a gallon

There was no running water into the house

When the little house out behind the house was the rest room, not a tool shed

The previous year's Montgomery Wards catalogue was used for toilet paper (it sure beat corn cobs)

When you milk the cows by hand in the rain in a thunderstorm

You walk in 3-4 feet of snow suddenly break through the crust and sink up to your crotch and get stuck there

When it seemed like the road was uphill on the way to school and back home

The best bicycle you have has a bent front fork so you have to time the pedal with the turn so your foot won't hit the front wheel.

You are away from the farm with a team of horses on a hay rack in a hail storm and the horses turn for home full speed ahead and go into the 3 foot wide barn door side by side at the same time with a wagon behind. UFFDA!!.

You have to plow the field with a team of horses instead of using a car like a Graham Paige?

You are asked to cultivate corn using a team of horses on a morning after the night before, when out on the town.

Getting home at 6 o'clock in the morning from an all-night Harvey Wallbanger party just in time to go to work. That'l learn me.

You have to milk the cows in the morning out in the rain again after being out on a Harvey Wallbanger party the night before.

The biggest cow of the herd of 13 was a hard milker anyway. She was so big she always got stuck in the mud so we had to go down with the Fordson tractor several times with 100 feet of barb wire (5-6 strands) and a log chain and wrap it around old Jim's neck and gently tug her out of the muddy ditch in the meadow and drag her onto dry land. Yah we called her Jim cow.

Every Saturday night was bath night for us kids weather we needed it or not. Usually we needed it. If we didn't smell from the dirt, mud, swamp mud, or barn manure, we just plain smelled. Before electricity was installed in the house Ma heated water on the wood stove and put it in a big round galvanized tub. She added some home-made soap and yelled "somebody get in." At that time there were 4 of us brats (3 boys, 1 girl). Obviously and luckily there was only room for 1 in the tub at a time. Thank goodness. We all smelled nice and fresh after that. I remember Ma always turned on that battery operated radio and listened to the Grand Ole Opry Ho Down music, bluegrass music and that good stuff until wee hours in the morning. You see, the Nashville radio station would turn up their power on Saturday nights and broadcast the Opry. There was Roy Acuff, Minnie Pearl and --- I loved that_____-kicking music and I still love it to this day.

CHAPTER 9

THE BIG WAR

Dad was 34 in 1942 and I remember he got a greeting card from Uncle Sam in the mail one day. Uncle Sam didn't want to talk about the weather or the stock market. He said "We want you". Of course Dad , the hard working guy that he was grabbed his acking back with one hand and the steering wheel with the other and drove faithfully down the road in the smoking '29 Chevrolet sedan with one door hanging half-way open and the tail pipe dragging to report for duty as requested.

Unless you've been there, you don't know how happy us kids were, and Ma too, when Dad came back home that day and said "I don't have to go to war because we are farming and got 3 rug rats so I don't have to go". Dad wasn't much of a kisser but I think he could have kissed the whole draft board that day.

But now Dad's Bro, my Uncle C received a greeting card too which said "We want you". Uncle C was a single man so they took him lock, stock and barrel. I think they even wanted his gun barrel cause there was a shortage of steel and the ammo plants were running overtime. Uncle was a hunter and a trapper of animals but a lover of people. He was a contentious objector—he wouldn't be able to shoot a man even in war and in my opinion that was all right too. Uncle C was the # 2 man in my life and at 6 years old I was glad about that. *Sorry about those tears in my eyes.*

Anyway, Uncle C received an Honorable Discharge. I have the papers and a folded United States Flag to remember him by. He's been there. He's gone now, up on the hill. Thank you American Legion for the presentation below.

An American flag presented to Uncle Carl S. Williams by the American Legion for honorable service

CHAPTER 10

THE BIG CITY

Meanwhile the Minnesota State Fair was on in the big city. It was the biggest and best fair in the whole country with 40 acres of machinery hill then, Midway rides, the 500 mile Labor Day stockcar races and large thick plants that were excellent places to hide and drink grape soda pop that we had found just stacked out behind the Church Dining Hall. It was so inviting.

Anyway me and a couple cousins (we'll call them Don B. and Billy B.) nearly got drunk on grape soda that night. Cousin Don had a rip in his pants, guess he got that when he got caught climbing over the 10 foot high barb wire fence. Don never did like paying admission at the State Fair gate. Maybe you remember Don. He's the guy that started me smoking corn silk when he was young?

Cousin Don at the State Fair wanted a foot long hotdog so he picked a wiener out of the hot water at the hotdog stand and literally measured it with his tape measure. Don's words were:

Don: "I want a foot long wiener dog".

Vendor: "OK".

Don: "this one is only 11-1/2 inches long". He then thru it back in the kettle after man handling it, squeezing it and mauling it till it almost fell apart.

Vendor: "No, don't do that".

Don: "Yes let me measure another one".

Anyway Don measured about 4 or 5 wieners before he found one that was 11-3/4 inches. He said "I'll take that one". What a guy. No dull moments with him around, let me tell you. I'm glad there is only one of him.

We sure had some good times. Some I prefer not to mention here. If I wrote about all the excitement during my life this book would never end. Yah, Been there. Did that. I remember. And now Billy is gone too.

As time went on in 1949 a neighbor guy ½ mile down the road, whom we'll call Johny, bought a hand tie Case hay baler and talked Dad into operating it doing custom baling for him. It took 3 people to operate the machine, one on the tractor, and two on the baler.

When we baled hay for his customers they usually would feed us supper if we were still working at supper-time. Supper in those days was the evening meal. Anyway, Johnnie arranged that with them cause he was tight, tight as a fiddle string, I mean real tight, so tight that he squeaked, In fact he was stingy tight, tighter than Dad's fiddle strings so he wanted us to make small loose bales for his customers but real large tight bales for himself.

Anyway this one particular customer gave us a good supper and the lady of the house, I think she ran the organization lock, stock and with a rifle barrel, asked if we would like a drink of her homemade dandelion wine. Dad not being much of a drinker of any alcohol said " OK, it sounds good". Well at the end of one of those crazy hay-baling days anything alcoholic sounded good. So the old gal poured Dad about a 8 oz glass full, me one 8 oz glass full and Bro Les about an 8 oz glass full. Well Dad must have been thirsty or something. He tipped that glass up, guzzled it down like it was the last liquid on earth. He barely got his glass back on the table and the sweat began to roll, I mean right now.

Dad said "wow that is good stuff". Right about now I had already taken a swig and the sweat was rolling, pouring, dripping like none other. Dad declined a second drink of her wine saying "somebody has to drive home". That was the best supper I've ever had at 15 years old.

Another baling job was for Tom H, a different Tom H. We were baling in the dark again and Tom was on the wagon stacking the bales as they came off the baler onto the wagon that was being pulled behind the baler. *If you aren't a farmer this may be complicated but please bare with me on this one and we'll get through it.*

Anyway as we turned a corner Tom walked to the front of the wagon toward the rear tractor lights, that's normal, but what wasn't normal was that the tractor lights were not straight ahead of the wagon cause we were making a turn and Tom didn't know that cause he was blinded by the tractor light and he walked right off the side of the wagon. Lucky he didn't get run over a couple times as we made a circle around to pick up some hay that was missed. I didn't realize we had lost Tom and Tom could hardly catch us cause we were heading out full steam ahead to make that big money, Oh yah. Some people's kids do the darndest things.

We tipped Johnnie's Coop tractor over one time, laid it right on the side in the muddy swamp. Johnnie didn't know that. We never told him. He never will cause he's gone now.

Anyway Johny paid Dad 4 cents per bale of hay that we baled for his customers. We bailed hay nearly every day all summer long, tens of thousands of bales. Fall came and good old Johnny came over to pay Dad for the summer's work. Now hold on to your hat cause Johnnie gave Dad a check for a whopping $100. Yah, $100. Dad surely was discussed. He took a look at us kids who had sweated and wiped the dust from our eyeballs with him all summer long, and he said "I don't think we will do it next year". That was enough of that baloney. Been there. Did that.

Us kids didn't want to loose the knack of backing up a farm wagon so we proceeded to do that for the rest of the fall.

Any one of us could back up a 4 wheel hay wagon hooked behind the F-12 Farmall tractor—up hill. I tried one wagon hooked behind another, 2 wagons in a row, up hill----- oh well.

CHAPTER 11

THE GOOD OL' 50's

The good old 50's when some people's kids did the craziest things.

By 1950 there were 8 of us rascals for Dad and Mom to feed. Even though they had 120 acres of land now only 80 acres were tillable. In 1951 Dad got hired at the Swift & Co packing plant down in the big city of South St. Paul.

Now I was going to high school (grades 9 thru 12) and doing the farming and milking 17 cows. Did you notice how our herd had multiplied in 10 years? The herd didn't multiply as fast as rabbits cause the neighbor's bull didn't jump the fence much so Dad's herd was pretty much inbreed and you know the rest.

Anyway Dad was always advancing with other stuff or something, even though he barely completed the 3rd grade in school he was a genius in my book.

Dad had advanced from a Fordson tractor to an F-12 Farm-All International so we felt we had the world by the tail once again. (US kids almost tipped that thing over too). By this time Dad again advanced to a Graham–Paige car, a 1929 model. It got a little lame on a few cylinders so Dad sold it to the local junk dealer man. He came with a big truck, rolled the Graham-Paige over on the roof and skidded it to town. If you ever heard a person cry, that was me. I was so mad cause we drove it a lot and played with it a lot. It had a big powerful engine and 4 speed trany that was geared down like a tractor. One time when Dad was gone us kids hooked the Graham to the plow and –man did we plow? We plowed dirt big time at 20 miles per hour across the field. Dad later wondered why the plow was acting weird. He said it seemed like it was bent or something. We never told him we had hooked a big freakin' rock at 20 MPH. He sort' a figured it out but really never will know.

Back in the high school days Dad drove to and from the big city stock yards every week end after he bought a real car—a 1937 Packard. He drove that back and forth to the cities at about 55 MPH until he bought a 1946 Mopar. Dad was the best. He gave me that Packard cause I did most of the farming. I quickly found out that Packard went 85 MPH rather than 55 mph like Dad had said.

Now me with the Packard, I had the world by the tail. One buddy (we'll call him eyeballs) had a '38 Olds, another (Willie) had a '37 Ford.

Saturday nights were a big deal in little towns in those days. All the stores were open till about 10: 00 P. M. The town was full of people. The stores were busy. People didn't have much money to spend but the stores were busy. Towns were meeting places on Saturday nights. Us kids usually went to the movie house theater —we could see Tarzan movie for 9¢. Then they went and raised it up to 12 ¢, then 15 ¢. (Inflation done hit!). That's back when Tarzan was played by Johny Weissmuller. Johny was the real Tarzan in my book.

Anyway us school kids, Eyeballs, Willie and guess who, who me would race? Would kind'a race our cars up and down mainstreet making squealing noises, double U-turns and that kind of stuff where U-turns should not be made. The old town constable said, "heh, you guys can't do that". We said " yes we can, just watch us" and we would do it again. The poor old man couldn't do much to us cause he didn't have a car, no gun, no club, not even a uniform. The best thing he had was his greasy bib overalls. Some people's kids referred to him as old black Sam. We weren't very nice. He was the same constable that almost caught somebody's kids throwing tomatoes onto mainstreet from on top of the lumber yard building on Saturday night when the band was playing "Yankee-Doodle". He was the same constable on duty the Saturday night that somebody's kids found some wiener dogs and smoked bacon in the back room of the local food store and they hung the wieners and bacon on a clothes line out back of the store. The bacon was kind'a chewy but the wiener dogs were delicious. It was the most published news in town since the previous decade. He didn't know that—he never will know that cause he's gone now too.

Anyway I eventually managed to graduate from High School in '54 (that was a miracle if there ever was one). Dad was the best of all Dads—he offered me the farm for next to nothing if I wanted it. By now it didn't take a rocket scientist to figure out what not to do. I said to Dad "Dad, I think I'll take a rain check" and I reminded Dad of the first time I saw the farm in1940 that day it was raining pitchforks and hammer handles?

My favorite Aunt and Uncle had about 9 rug rats and had been renting the farm for a while and I knew they wanted to buy it so I told Dad I didn't want to farm. Dad sold them the farm. I remember cause I've Been there and I Did that.

CHAPTER 12

AFTER HIGH SCHOOL

Like father, like son I went to N. D., that's North Dakota (some say it "Nordakoda"), to work summer harvest. (I not knocking North Dakota, after all I was born there, in the Turtle Mountains and they do have some trees, some places).

I worked for a farmer and nearly tipped over the guy's cattle truck going downhill. Would you believe the darn brakes gave out? Of course I was hauling cattle instead of horses and you probably know that cattle don't stand up very well in a moving truck going downhill around a curve at 60 MPH like horses will. Cattle flop over real easy and lay down on the job. Anyway to my surprise I made it to the bottom in fair condition, a little shaky, but fair, and the cattle? Well they were OK too. This happened one morning after the night out before, if you know what I mean. I never told the farmer about that close call. He never knew. He never will know. He's gone now too.

And I worked for a grain farmer out there too. Had a good time and an adventurous time to say the least. I was working the field driving a D4 cat with 23 foot wide disk and a 23 foot wide drag behind the disk going across a mile long dirt field that was flat as a cow chip on a rock. All of a sudden, I mean sudden, the front end of the caterpillar went down and then suddenly it went up. Somehow this got my attention and woke me up real fast. Don't recall how long I had been sleeping but I had Been there. Did that. I remember.

Anyway I dosed off and I had just run off into the ditch, up onto the road. I hastily grabbed the right clutch lever, pushed hard on the right hand brake. Man you should of seen the disk, drag and the caterpillar whip around over the road and down into the ditch on the other side and finally back up on top the road and then straightened out when I got back on the field that belonged to the farmer I was working for. Amazingly I never heard any percussion about the episode. The only reason I can figure out how all this happened was that this was the morning after the night before. You see my buddy and I had gone to town the night before and had a couple drinks of Sunny Brook Special (a couple pint bottles that is) and barely got back to our respective bunkhouses in time for breakfast. This was where I learned to eat rare steak. You see, meals were part of the work deal. Breakfast (if I made it home in time), dinner at noon time, and supper at evening time were on time and if I weren't there it was my tough luck. So one evening the man called me for supper. We all sat down and started passing food around and the Misses said " I'll put the steak in the oven". Wholy moly I thought to myself, what did she say? Well anyhow in about 4 minutes she pulled them steaks out of the oven and handed the platter to me first. I loved steak but wasn't sure if I wanted to try this one. I mean it was red, juicy, still wiggling and barely warm on the top. Proceeded to cut it up and fake it a little while eating it. The Misses said "is there something wrong"? I said "NO" and kept picking at it. Well that was that and I had raw steak several times after that.

Anyway that's a couple of my North Dakota work experiences. The farmer never knew that I nearly wrecked his disk, drag and caterpillar tractor. He never will know. He's gone now too! Been there. Did that. I remember.

CHAPTER 13

Eagle Bend 1950's-1960's

Eagle Bend in the 50's and 60's was the busiest little town in central Minnesota aside from Bertha, Hewitt, Clarissa, Verndale, Wadena, Staples and a few others. I'm not tellin' you how old I am but when I was a kid in the 40's this little town was bouncing every week day night and twice on Saturday nights. The ballroom at Clarissa was bouncing on Saturday night until wee hours of the morning. Clarissa didn't have enough restaurant space after the dance so Eagle Bend was the busy hangout that got invaded by the "after hours happy people". I think the owner of the E B café was glad to see us leave so he could close up for the night. The sidewalks didn't close until at least 10:30 or 11:00 in the evening and 2:00 or so A.M. on Saturday night.

I didn't have any problem in this little town cause I knew Mr. Ed the Policeman here. He was a normal man, he helped people instead of giving them hell. We didn't do squealing, double U-Turns on main street here cause Ed was a likable guy.

And we baled hay for Ed on his farm too but he didn't walk off the edge of the bale wagon like his Bro Tom did. You remember Tom? He walk off the bale wagon in the dark and nearly got run over.

I had been driving a car since I was 15, right or wrong, I was driving. I was testing Dads car. I pretended I was a test driver and I liked to confirm that they really went faster than Dad always said. Eagle Bend was one of our speed ways.

I just loved to race the '37 Packard then, not only on the road but in the hay field. This one time I was going across the field to-beat- the-band to head off the cows, which was legitimate because they were out of the pasture and going into the good neighbors crop.

Well wouldn't you know, all of a sudden it seems like this very, very big rock just jumped out of the tall grass right in front of me? That old Packard went up and over that baby like a bucking bronco and came to a sudden halt when the front end dug into the dirt. The left front "A" frame had gotten beat up so bad that it didn't resemble an "A" frame at all. I had to walk home and obviously Dad asked "what happened." I said " the steering went bad or something. Yah, that's what it was. The steering went bad" I said. "The steering went bad". Anyway Dad picked up the pieces and took them to the local blacksmith shop man whom we will call Lee. He straightened it out like new and stuff and Dad continued letting me drive it.

Later on Dad gave me that Packard and I drove the heck out of it. The engine started burning so much oil I would go to the full service station and tell the attendant to check the gas and fill it up with oil. It still burnt so much oil I thought I'd fix that deal so I put in some # 90 weight oil. That didn't burn so fast but it didn't lube the bearings properly and I thru a rod bearing in the engine. As mentioned earlier, I traded it off that same day, in the "as is" condition cause I really needed a car to go to town that night. Didn't want to miss anything, you know?

Yeah those were the good old days.

AND THEN TIMES CHANGED

CHAPTER 14

JACKSON AND THE TOWN THAT WAS

And then times changed when a recession came in the 70's and 80's and it seemed like the sidewalks rolled up at 6:00 in the evening. Many of the old timers were pushing daisies up on the hill.

What once was a prosperous little German and Norwegian town – Yah Shuer- dwindled down to a gas station on the highway, three or four churches, a café or two and the senior citizens center. I imagine the senior citizen center may close soon cause there aren't many seniors left.

What once was a prosperous Co-op creamery where Dad sold milk now has a sign on the door "Closed until further notice". There was no further notice. The brick building is boarded up and is beginning to crumble from the cold Minnesota Winters.

Eagle Bend Creamery

The C o-op grocery, clothing and everything else store where Ma sold eggs put a sign on the front door "Closed for business until further notice". I have not seen any further notice.

The Co-op store where Ma sold eggs

She sold as many as three or four 60 dozen cases every other day. We would watch them cantle the eggs by holding them up by a light to grade them and check to see that there were not any little chicks in them, and to see if they were good quality and size before they paid Ma.

The Co-op gas station that was located nearby where Ma and Dad bought gas if they had any money left after groceries had a sign on the door "Closed until further notice". There has been no further notice.

The Co-op feed store is where Ma bought feed for the chickens cause the farm wasn't large enough to grow enough grain. It was coming to be another vicious cycle. Farming wasn't very prosperous unless you had hundreds of acres and a lot of money.

The feed store is no longer the Co-op store. There has been no further notice.

The Co-op Feed Store

It looks like the old Co-op feed store is leaning to the west unless I was leaning because I took this picture on a morning after the night before.

Us kids used to grow one or two acres of cucumbers and sell pickles at the local town pickle factory. We'd break our back every day picking cucumbers. It was our spending money. It wasn't much but it was something. The pickle factory was located west of the Co-op Feed Store near the railroad tracks. One day we picked and hauled in several feed sacks full of prime size pickles to town and saw a sign on the pickle factory door "Closed until further notice". We never saw any further notice.

A little later the blacksmith shop where Dad had Blacksmith Lee make that blacksmith-made scooter for us kids had a sign on the door "Closed until further notice". To this day there is no mention of a further notice.

The town's only drug store had a supply of necessities from band-aids to horse pills and everything in between. The older people died off and so did the demand for drugs. So Virgil put a sign on the door "Closed until further notice". He pulled up his pants and suspenders and hobbled down to the corner pool hall and played cards with the old folks.

And then there was the local town scrap man dealer, junk man if you will. Everybody called him "Skinny". Skinny was the guy in our deer hunting gang that never got lost cause he coughed so bad everybody could find him in the woods at any time. I believe he never got one deer in all the years he hunted. I think he had that all planned too. He got an equal share of meat anyway cause Dad was that way— everybody got an equal amount of venison even if they didn't shoot one down. He was the guy that Dad had to come and hook on the Graham-Paige car and drag it to town cause the engine got so worn out it wouldn't start and parts were getting hard to find. Skinny didn't close the door to his junk yard cause he didn't have a door. He just died and everything rusted away.

Skinnie's Junk Yard with Skinny in the center

The town theatre where Dad took us kids to see Tarzan movie on Saturday nights put a sign on the ticket window "Closed until further notice." There has been no further notice that Tarzan would be coming to town. The building is now occupied by the fire department.

The country schools closed so kids are bused to the town schools.

Country churches closed one by one. Yeah Surer. As old folks passed away, one by one, the small funeral parlors closed and consolidated into one.

Then the small town high schools consolidated and time went on.

If this is any consolation, two things are guaranteed –taxes and death. Thank God some of the churches are still active but the cemeteries are getting full.

The last time I drove through the town I saw a lonely elderly man on mainstreet walking slowly toward the senior citizen's center.

I walked up to him and said "are you ok?"

He said "yeah I'm ok."

I said "may I ask your name?"

"I am Mr. Jackson" he said.

Anyway Jackson was the only person on the street. We talked and talked and talked about where everybody was at.

I said "Mr. Jackson, where is everybody"?

"Well", he said "they are resting up on the hill, up by your Mom and Dad. I remember your Dad when he was younger cause he worked for me in my garage fixing cars and stuff. You see, most people couldn't afford new cars so we were busy with car fixing."

I said "nice talking to you, Mr. Jackson, you have a great day and take care".

Mr. Jackson cleared his throat and slowly limped down main street to the senior citizen center only to find it closed for the day. Sure it was Sunday but Sunday was a big day for the seniors to gather around, play cards, chat a bit about the weather, about the crops (or about the crops that weren't).

I drove by the old farm to see how everything was. That was the 40 acres that Dad had bought in the brush on that day in 1940 when it rained pitchforks and hammer handles.

I drove into the yard like I owned the place. A man came out of the house and said "could I help you".

"Well, I am Gene and I am just looking around, I used to live here when I was a kid".

60

He said "just call me Luke". We just talked and talked and talked about how things have changed. I told him the thing about how that first part of the first house that used to be right here where we are standing had got here. He seemed amazed and smiled a little. I could see that he knew there was tears in my eyes as big as you know what when I turned the other way. I think he was saying to himself "I am sorry that I changed this place so much".

I said "you have a good day, I need to go now".

Yes things had changed. The original house (the one room house with a bed sheet across the middle to make a two room house that Dad had the road grader man pull on the road from Norway Grandma's homestead) was gone. I saw a new one built up in the woods. The barn, the shed, and the other sheds are gone. And the all important outhouse with the Montgomery Wards catalogues are gone. The orchard that Ma had out by the road is no longer there. It is now farm land. The old cart trail road that went by the farm in 1939 is now a real road with gravel and ditches along side and a street sign reading 400th ST.

The good neighbor that lived a mile down the road or ¾ mile the way the crow flied across the swamp had moved away. They were the "Eggs" family. There is now a new house there, and new people there. The only old thing I remember that is still there is the old silo by the barn, the barn that used to be there. The Eggs family had a real silo. Dad's silo was snow fence stacked one on top of another as we filled the area with corn stocks chewed up with a silo filler machine. I'm not sure where Dad got the snow fence from. Maybe he knew somebody important on the highway department or maybe just borrowed the fence, temporarily of course.

CHAPTER 15

Bertha, MN the 50's & 60's

Back in the good old days during the '50's and '60's the local café and bar was doing very well considering some peoples kids bombarded it too, and gave owner/operator Joe a bad time cause he wouldn't serve us beer after 2:00AM.

The movie theatre was crowded and going full blast, especially when a Tarzan movie was playing.

The little home-style bakery was selling dozens and dozens of fresh goodies every day especially at noon time on school days. It was located about 4 city blocks from the high school and some of us would run over and buy 3 rolls, bismarks, donuts, whatever for 10 ¢ . Yes, 3 for one thin dime. Noon lunch at the school cafeteria cost us 15¢ a day but it didn't satisfy me.

The creamery was going full blast and they made butter and ice cream that was "out of this world", sorta' speak. The price was right too.

Grandma Gutman's, everybody called her Grandma, ice cream shop had the best in town and sometimes we had to wait in line to get a cone but it was worth waiting for.

The Golden Rule general store on the corner across from the bank was always busy with bargains on everything from soup to nuts, clothing, odds and ends and everything in between. It was like the Macy's of Bertha.

The implement dealer was doing fairly well selling Minneapolis Moline tractors and stuff.

In 1953 the high school was added on to accommodate the population explosion in the neighboring towns.

The local town bank was borrowing money to farmers and businesses when they needed it.

The 3 gas stations were all busy and gas was around 20¢ to 23 ¢ a gallon. (I tried to burn farm gas in the '37 Packard but Dad said we can't do that cause the government wouldn't like it. It was a farm-free tax thing.)

The little city hospital was open 24/7, if you knock on the door hard, and was available for emergencies for people like me when the back wheel came off the tractor cause I fell asleep and didn't pay attention to driving. It was one of those days after the night before, you know what I mean?

DR. Will the only dentist in town was busy. Ma took us kids to him cause he was the cheaper between here and E. B. The reason I remember him was he never used any Novocain when he drilled teeth for fillings and we had a lot of fillings. The worst part was his hands shook like he was mixing a milk shake until his drill thing and his hand got into the mouth, then he calmed down. Those old style drills smelled and burned, burned the skin especially when he slipped and gouged the jaw bone. They were so noisy that they sounded like a 10 ton truck grinding it's way up a hill. No lie.

This was a busy little town that hopped on Saturday nights when all the stores were open for business. Everybody visited on the streets and talked about the conditions on the farms. No body blabbed, it was no paton place. Everybody basically minded their own business but they were friendly. The town had their own theatre and their own funeral parlor.

This was where some people's kids came to race and play. This was another one of our drag strips, another test strip. This is where some people's kids used to terrorize the city constable, day and night. He was the constable that had no gun, no car, no uniform, no billy club. Those black marks on the street may be some of ours.

This is the street where somebody's kids found some bacon strips and weiner dogs and sausages in the back end of the food store and hung them on the cloths line out back of the store. (the door was open, so---).

And that's the way it was. But then things changed.

CHAPTER 16

THE RECESSION-1970's-1980's

As time went on in the '80's businesses began to close one by one. The Saturday night band and street parades came to a halt and there are no more. (that's the parades that got bombarded with juicy ripe tomatoes that somebody's kids threw down from the top of the lumber yard). I recall one time a big juicy tomato went right into the tuba horn. That was messy. UFFDA! The horn sound changed to a low bellering gurgle and we got our butts off that roof and out of town double time.

Bertha Creamery

The last time I drove thru town there was a sign on this creamery door too. The sign read "Closed until further notice". We have seen no further notice.

The Golden Rule Store

The Golden rule store was "Closed until further notice".

And now the high school where I graduated from appears to be closed until further notice.

Grandma Gutman's ice cream shop "Closed until further notice" and is now gone.

Formerly Frownies Café & Bar

This is the bar on main street that owner Joe kicked us out of and wouldn't serve us kids beer after 2:00 AM. I told him "we have been kicked out of better places". And now a sign on the door says "Closed, For Sale".

A sign was seen on the theatre ticket booth "Closed until further notice". There has been no further notice.

The gas station on the corner on main street, (that's the corner that eyeballs and me did the double U turns squeeling our tires and all that stuff) had a sign on the front "Closed until further notice". I am not holding my breath for a further notice.

The bank on the corner is closed and has been turned into a Museum that is seldom open. The implement dealer moved out on the highway in an attempt to catch some customers.

And "that's the way it is". I've Been there. Did that. I remember.

AND NOW

PART TWO:

SOME PEOPLE'S KIDS DID THE CRAZIEST THINGS

CHAPTER 17

THINGS GOT BETTER LIKE MA SAID

Ma always said "things will get better some day". Well, things got better and some people's kids did the craziest things.

I operated a backhoe digging machine a couple times. Yah I was asked to dig a trench between a barn and a house and lay a water line. Well here in Minnesota a water line needs to be about seven feet down so it won't freeze in the winter. I know, you probably ask "what the heck you doing in that cold weather"? That's a fair question. If it wasn't Minnesota I could of got by with a 16 inch deep trench and everything would have been safer. What I mean is I hoed the wrong thing, when sparks flew all over and I got a tickle up my spine it didn't take a rocket scientist to figure it out that somehow I had hooked someone's buried power line. There's only one thing more exiting and more jolting than that, that is trying to catch a lightning bolt with your bare hands.

We had a motorcycle once. Not just any motorcycle--but a Harley Davidson 74 hog, a 1949. I called it "Harley". That's the first year that Harley came out with a hydro glide fork? Anyway it didn't last long after I cracked it up.

I still called it a "Harley" but buddy Tom called it hardly a Harley after that.

I did a complete wheelie with 74 Harley. I had to check my pants to see if I did a stoolie shortly after that. As Les would say "That's copa-static".

I like to keep things short so to keep this story short—us guys, bro Les, Tom, Wayne and silly me went to a cycle confiscation course, a hill climb event. Les had a Harley Sportster all set up for hill climbing events. Well after one of the hill climbing events Tom H. says " hey why don't we go around the course like the others did? Well, dumb me said "ok" so I followed Tom, Wayne followed me, Les followed up the rear. We continued to go faster each time around. Wayne was pushing me to go faster and faster. Dumb me—I went faster and faster.

Well after about 3 times around the course I got braver and braver. I came down this one hill like all get-out and when I got to the bottom I swear somebody had dumped a load of fine sand on the trail. This sand was so fine and loose like powder that my bike fish-tailed back and forth, up and down a few times and the front end came up like a rearing horse and according to the spectators I made two loopidy loops in the air and landed against a window on a Mopar station wagon. I was ok, sorta', but that Harley didn't look the same as when I started.

The headlight laid 50 feet from the scene. That hydro glide fork looked a little squiggly and bent and twisted. The windshield was busted to smithereens. The motor knocked like none other ever did. I landed upside down, slapped against that Mopar station wagon. I haven't driven a wild Harley since. The best part was, I wasn't drinking. Maybe I should have had a few Harvey Wallbangers or Elmer Fudpuckers then I would have had an excuse for my silly actions and what I did.

Like I say "I'm not responsible for my actions after 8:00 at night. If you want the whole truth, I'm not responsible for my actions before 8:00 at night". This maybe was another one of those mornings after the night before.

Anyway on the way home that day the Harley started knocking like I never heard before. A couple days later the engine locked up tight. End of Harley.

CHAPTER 18

CRAZY THINGS

I never did any crazy things but did have some close calls beyond my control. A buddy of mine (we'll call him #1 Normal Bruce) and myself were flying by air to a job site. Bruce was in charge of the job and he wanted to keep the cost low by flying 2 legs rather than a direct flight. Well wouldn't you know the 2nd leg was by a little 2 motor prop job plane from Nashville to Augusta. Anyway on this little 20 seated plane there was a little lady from somewhere in the Tennessee boondocks (we could tell by her accent). She was nice and friendly and asked if we fly much and ever had any close calls. I told her yes we fly a lot and once in a while an engine catches fire but that's about all. She began to shake a little and got all nervous so I told her we've got used to it by now. By now she was getting really nervous and worried and more shaky.

About now the pilot announced that he had an engine going out and would have to make an emergency landing in Knoxville. Like I say, let me tell you, this Tennessee lady looked back at me and said "what did he say?" The pilot said it again and that lady went completely hysterically berserk. She almost jumped over the back of the seat onto my lap. (About now I had to remind her that I was married). Anyway when I told her to uncover her eyes so she could see the smoking engine better she got worse, really worse, really wild I mean. We finally landed, well sort'a, Ok. That lady was shacking when she got off the plane. She said, I ain't never going to fly again".

So we got on the next plane (it was another little 2 motor prop job) that was headed for Augusta. Bruce said "where is the Tennessee lady"? I said " I don't know, I saw her going into the rest room a while back and she never came out and I ain't going in there to check on her. Are you"? Anyway she never got on the next flight to her destination. We never saw her or heard from her again. Been There. It did happen. I Remember!

CHAPTER 19

KOREA AND THE WAR

A buddy that I worked with (we'll call him Mel) was in that war. He really didn't want to talk about it. He clammed up when I mentioned it but one day he opened up. Mel said "how would you feel if you were along side your best buddy and bullets flying all around and all of a sudden you don't see your buddy so you turn and look back. You see him laying 20 feet behind you in a pool of blood, his guts are not where they are supposed to be, his rifle had the bayonet extended, the bayonet is stuck in the ground beside him, his testicles are draped neatly over the butt of the rifle". Mel continued "that was the war, 20 feet behind me".

I was fortionate compared to that. I was in after the hot part, after the so-called truce? It was supposed to be peace time but that was only words spoken on Freedom Bridge. We could see Freedom Bridge from camp, a stone's throw away. We could almost see the whites of Joe Chink's eyes as he marched along the border and mumbled a few words as if he was not a happy camper.

Anyway I drove a duce and- a -half in our army in South Korea until I almost laid it on the side. You see, we were supposed to drive only on roads and in rice patties but it was more fun trying to drive up "pork chop hill". The government wanted me to get an army drivers license and then sign for a truck and be responsible for it's condition. Well I declined all that baloney and stuff, flatly refused. Maybe that's why I never made any rank after that. I never lost any rank either, only had one stripe and tried to keep that for a backup just in case I got caught off limits or something similar.

It was more interesting to go off limits where we could see how the people really lived in 8 ft by 8 ft clay huts with grass roofs with a brush fire under the stone floor for heating.

Anyway I managed to hang on to that one precious PFC stripe. I believe what helped me there was one night on guard duty up by the Demilitarized Zone, DMZ, the chicken _____ officer of the day came prowling around the bushes in the dark. All I could see was a silhouette of a person.

The officer of the days always said "be sure you can recognize a person that may be near you. You need to be sure you can see him or her clearly. If you can't , ask them to halt". I thought I recognized his voice when he said he was the officer of the day but couldn't be sure so I said "halt". He didn't stop so I said "halt".

Well the halt conversation wasn't working so I said "get down on the ground or I will shoot, get flat on your face or else". He argued, I argued, he argued again, I argued some more. Finally he realized I wasn't bluffing. Well normally we only had blank amo but that day they had issued us some live amo cause there was a rumor that Joe from North Korea may be coming across the border tonight to pay us a visit and the visit was not to talk about the weather.

So now—the officer knew I might be serious and he went down flat on the ground in the mud. I purposely halted him near the mud puddle cause I had no love for this guy. Anyway I walked over to him and recognized him behind that muddy face with his shiny brass, his 2nd John bar, polished boots, starched uniform and all that stuff. I said "sorry sir", I saluted him and allowed him to get up. He looked all mad, hypered, confused and yes all messy and still muddy but he said "Good job done".

After that episode I went to the mess hall for breakfast. The food in the mess hall was atrocious as usual.The main cook had no experience in cooking whatsoever. He had a mechanic's MOS/certification instead of cooking experience. Furthermore, he didn't like to cook so most of the food was burned. I mean really burned to a crisp. None of us G.I.'s were fond of black fried eggs. He tried cooking eggs, he tried frying eggs, he tried poaching eggs, he tried boiling eggs, he tried scrambling eggs, he tried it all but in the end they still all looked the same burned black. I think one time he didn't turn the heat on the pan of bacon cause it was cold and raw as sin.

Some of us guys asked the captain for a transfer if we couldn't get better food. The captain said "if you transfer you'll be going up by the front lines". Well that was nothing new cause we were already at the front line and could see the North Korean soldiers on the Freedom Bridge. We were so close that we could see the enemy loading their rifles and they had real live bullets with lead in them. I assume they didn't know we had blank bullets or they would of run us over even though there was a signed truce. They were not happy looking people. They just weren't happy at all.

We weren't real happy that day either. We would sooner be at the "tin hut bar" as I called it, soaking up a couple Korean Joe-Joe beers or a snort of Korean whiskey even though it tasted like gasoline. Or we could have been down in the local village shooting words with Papason even though he couldn't understand a word we said and we couldn't understand one word he was saying. I eventually learned some of the language like the stuff that wasn't real nice. That was the easiest to learn, it sort'a came natural. Did I say that?

PAPASON WITH HIS A-FRAME

There were some good things about Korea in the '50's but I don't know where they were. If you have been there you know what I mean.

If you haven't been there—imagine a person going potty in the stream on the village street and then down-stream somebody is scooping water from that same stream and drinking it. Imagine people roasting a dog over a fire on the ground with fur and head and all the stuff still all together.

More than once we saw a dog get hit by an army jeep and you never in a life-time see the people run so fast to claim that dead dog. Everybody ran to get that dead dog—some young kids, mamason, papason, even gramason. This one old grandma started running toward the dog and she stumbled on something, rolled a few times and feel right on top of the dead dog like a football player tackling a football. Laugh? Anyway they had to eat something and the price was right. They raised very few pigs for food and I never found out why that was. Their cattle were pretty skinny and were used for work animals to pull wagons and plows and stuff. The cattle were sacred and I respect that.

Back to the dogs—as far as I could see some of them ate every part of the dog including the skin and the head. I ate dog meat one time but remember I'm not responsible for my actions after 8:00 PM? You see I had slopped down a few beers and topped it off with a couple glasses of booze down in the village. This one lady was eating some soup and she asked if I wanted some. Well to my better judgment I said "yes why not". She brought me some in what looked like a clean bowl and a pair of chop sticks. There were veggies, meat and some unknown ingredients in a good looking liquid. The meat was sliced and really tender and tasted like pork so I didn't hesitate. Anyway I ate it all and asked for more until I was told that the meat was dog meat. That cured me temporarily.

CHAPTER 20

CHICKEN BONES & BUFFETS

I enjoy food--especially Cajun and Chinese buffets. I ordered a ½ buffet one time but they wouldn't accept my order. The manager said " we don't have ½ buffets". I told him "well I only plan on eating half as much as I usually do". It didn't work, it went in one ear and out the other and they charged me full price anyway. I said to myself "self, I'll learn 'em" and I ate twice what I normally did. I guess they thought I was born just yesterday!

As I mentioned before-some people eat to live, I live to eat. Chinese buffets are my favorite. Chicken is one of my favorites, any color, in any size, shape or form. It had been said that my truck tasted like chicken? I think they meant it smelled like chicken. OK so I did find chic bones under my seat several times. I guess most people have one vice or so. (my vice was eating chicken while driving). I used to eat peanuts in my '65 Dodge all the time too. I was known as peanut man on the CB radio after they discovered peanut shells all over the car floor. The only thing harder to clean up from the car floor was oysters mixed with broken glass after that incident when those two guard rails moved right in front of me one evening after a social party which I prefer not to mention all the details for the host's sake.

Bottineau grandma used to give us kids coffee when we were young. She would put a lot of milk in it so maybe Ma wouldn't notice we were drinking coffee. Ma said it would stunt our growth. Man was she right!! I only got to 5'- 8 ½ " at tallest. Now I'm 5'-7 ½ ". What's going on here? Guess it's all moving down and sprawling out. Now I'm all belly and no hips.

And now some people say my coffee tastes like battery acid. I drink strong coffee but I met my match for strong coffee in New Orleans (the locals there call it Nawleens).Been there. Did that. I remember. And I sure am going to miss that place.

CHAPTER 21

JACK OF ALL TRADES

I've had a lot of different jobs in my lifetime. I was kind of a jack-of-all-trades, a master of none. I didn't even master the art of drinking alcohol so start with---------

Start with farmer, mechanic, machinist, meat cutter, bowling ball pinsetter, dishwasher, nursery worker, pea vinery pea pitcher, carpenter, well driller, inspector and retired person. I think I have the retired person part pretty well mastered.

Oil ran all over the machine shop floor one night. The turning lathe tools got hot and nearly wrecked everything cause the oil on the floor wasn't lubricating where it was supposed to. Maybe this happened cause of the fun I had the night before and this was a morning after?

The mechanic thing was a no-brainer for me. When I was 15 years old I replaced a clutch plate in the '37 Packard outside in the snow bank at 20 degrees below zero (that's a minus 20 F) cause I was determined to go to town that night. I had $5 and it was Saturday night. That was when the economy was still fairly good and the town didn't roll up the sidewalk at 6:00 PM.

We won't talk much about the meat-cutting job. I lost control of my knife, completely missed the mesh glove and cut the wrong meat-- real bad. After being laid up a long while because of another morning after the night before learned me. I don't drink no more—and no less except once in a while.

This is hard to believe but the bowling pin setting and dish washing went almost flawless. That's scary.

Somehow I nearly wrecked the 1942 John Deere tractor and my leg. Guess I feel asleep on this job too. The right rear tractor wheel came off all of a sudden (these sudden things had a way of happening) off the axel and rolled out in to the field. I was going full blast about 20 MPH when it happened. The tractor was ok. I was laid up again for a while cause the spline shaft was turning on my ankle as it laid across the edge of the road. (This was the same ankle that I sprained in Korea that night before I was supposed to go home, due to a couple too many beers). And now some people call me "the 2 beer kid".

That was the same John Deere tractor that caught on fire when cousin Don, and yah, my sister put gas in it when the motor was running. Kids, don't try that at home! Anyway I didn't tell Dad I fell asleep at the controls. He will never know.

Working at the local tree nursery was different too. My buddy (let's call him Wayne) always played around and stuff, a real cut-up kid, stepping on seedlings and I remember the foreman's remarks with a broken accent "foughteen cents each, (he tried to say that 14 cents each was the cost of the seedlings). Wayne would mock him and cut up some more. How could I not remember him? And he's not gone yet.

Now the pea vinery job-- that too was different. Four of us guys (Bro Les, Wayne, his bro Tom and myself) got the job with the legendary Minnesota Giant canning company one summer. We thought we could afford to work there by riding our motorcycles to the job site. We all had Harleys except Wayne, he had just a regular motorcycle. We were making right around $1.35 an hour. They had a bonus system so Bro Les and myself said to myself "self--let's try to make their bonus." So we decided to pitch peas until our butts dragged to make a bonus. Ok so we pitched peas 12 -16 hrs/day, seven days a week for 2 weeks until our butts dragged. Finally got our paycheck and noticed we had made a bonus of something like a buck -two-ninety eight, that's $1.98 and a little tiny bit more. I looked at Les, Les looked at me and all 4 of us took off down the road and never returned again. Been there. Did that. I remember.
But Tom said "I gotta' find a job cause the wife shops at Needless Mark-up and Dilly Bar stores". So Tom went down the road as fast as that bike could go.

Tom was my best friend and was always up to pulling some kind of a shenanigan. He electrified the foil strips in his living room couch one time and sent me straight up in the air when I sat on it. He just laughed and let one of those smelly lima bean smells slide out again. Tom was always eating Lima beans which never did him any good. In fact they gave him a bad smell and he would always laugh about it. Tom and I stopped for a nickel cup of coffee one time on University Avenue in the big city. Man you should of heard Tom holler when the coffee cost us $1.25 a cup. Anyway Tom borrowed me his '56 Ford one time to go on a trip that I will never forget. We hit a couple pheasants with it but Tom got over it. In my book Tom was the best, next to Les. Tom is gone now and that's kind' scary.

The carpenter work fiasco was a fiasco. Sometimes I hit the wrong nail and got beat-up hands to prove it.

Another real professional job was well drilling. This rig has seen it's better days.

Oh, Yah!!I only tipped the 38 foot tall rig over one time. Laid it right on the side, in the field. I worked drilling with my father-in-law too. He was a swell guy and he liked his booze. Sometimes him and I would go to the local joint for noon lunch and stuff. It usually ended up being stuff and no lunch. Well they didn't have lunches there except liquid lunch. Anyway we would have a couple or so until maybe 3:00

PM, then have one for the road and have a pint on the way home. Sure couldn't beat him for a boss.

One of his old drillers that we'll call Lloyd, a good old Swede he was, he would give you the shirt off his back anyway, even a swig from his bottle and he always had a bottle.

One day him and I were drilling a well and he came out from the truck, nearly stumbled over himself and said "Cheney I just heard the most beautiful music coming from under the dash of the truck and I caught every note of it". Well, there was no radio in the truck so take it from there--I was beginning to get concerned. He stumbled over to the rig and started talking to my father-in-law down the hole and he asked me which hole I was drilling in. Now that really began to bother me big time. I told him I was drilling in the hole that the tools were hanging in.

Anyway that seemed to satisfy him momentarily until he started talking to the boss down the well casing. He said the boss Tom, (we'll call him Tom) answered him back. Well to make this short, Tom was some 40 miles away. Now it didn't take a rocket scientist to figure it out that I was now really bothered and concerned so I told Lloyd let's call it a day and I took him home.

The next day his wife put him in detox, again. Another time his wife put him in there cause he claimed he saw a bunch of pink elephants going across the road in front of him so close that he had to slow down to prevent hitting any. Well to the best of my knowledge we never, ever had pink elephants running loose in Minnesota. The boss took him home that morning.

Lloyd used to stop at the local gas station and shoot the breeze and tell stories. He was a real story teller anyway. Well one day he was tending the gas pumps alone and some goof ball robbed him and shot him in the guts. He's gone now. We heard tell that the killer confessed several years later. That'l learn him.

Meanwhile my in-law boss Tom needed to get a piece of the old skow drilling rig (that was what he called the old Howell well-drilling rig) welded. We went to an old stone building in town and got the owner whose name was Pinkie to weld the piece. Pinkie was a man of few words but his actions were real. When we asked if he could fix the part he said "Well I don't know if I can get it done today". Then he walked over to his big acetylene torch, dug for his torch lighter, put a big cigar in his mouth, lit the torch and then lit his cigar from the torch, put out the torch, rolled up the torch hose, took a couple puffs and said "I'll have it fixed in 20 minutes". That was Pinkie.

MEAT PACKING BUDDIES—

During the days of the crew-cut and greasy hair oil I seldom got a haircut. One day at work a buddy at the packing plant (we'll call him Wild Bill) took up a collection from the gang to get Will a haircut. He called me Will. So Wild Bill got a quite large collection, took me to the barber, I got a haircut and Bill and I went to the local bar and drank 10 or 12 boiler makers on the rest of the money. (That'll learn'em).

Guess you know what a boiler -maker is!! Right?" Well back then it had more punch than a Harvey Wall Banger and an Elmer Fud Pucker combined. We did this at our favorite bar where we went for several years. One time I told the owner of that joint "let's have a drink I'm 21 today". That went over like a lead balloon and bar owner Joe wasn't so friendly anymore. He's gone now.

Wild Bill's better half wanted to go up North one time with their big 1956 Buick and Bill simply said to her "go ahead, here's a quarter for gas".

Now that Boston Blacky guy as everybody in the plant called him--he was really different, I'd say. He was originally from Boston I guess but that was no excuse. He was so stingy, tight and unpredictable from one day to the next. He was single at first, OK? He played the stock markets. He would find a newspaper in the locker room and check the stock markets daily and took only $20 a week from his pay to live on to cover room, food, gas everything. The rest went into stocks. We could tell how the stock markets were doing on any given day by his attitude. He would be real mad and owly if the markets went down. He was so tight he made soup from the same turkey bones over and over 6 times. That was before he got married.

Boston attempted to run a knife in me one time at work. He was big and tall, strong as an ox and grabbed me by the collar and held me in the air telling me he was going to cut me. Well I couldn't do anything so I just called his bluff by saying "well go right ahead and get it over with". That ain't no lie.

He was so stingy and said no woman would ever get a hold of him. Well I've heard that one before. And so she did. She was the most beautiful thing you ever saw, about 21 at most. Boston was 40 at the time. Well anyway she corralled him hook, line, sinker and money, lock, stock and barrel, Literally the money. It was over for him and his $$ signs. She finally divorced him after he insisted making another batch of turkey soup from the same bones after they were married. Boston Blacky is gone now. Thank goodness there was only one of him.

NDT, nondestructive testing was the best job in my life until now. I went back to school at 49 years young. I quit smoking then cause I wouldn't be able to go into the lab areas so I said to myself, "self I got to quit". Now if my memory serves me right (I know that's scary) I had to spend twice the time cracking the books and stuff as the young guys did. The NDT allowed me to venture into automated ultrasonics in Houston, Tx. My opinion of Houston is--------. I agree with the TV commercial that says "come to Texas, it's like another country". Anyway I traveled to about 40 of the states, plus Porto Rico and Taiwan.

A typical daytime scene in Houston is a pan handler on a corner with a sign beside him that read "HELP, God bless". There were she pan handlers as well as he pan handlers some were sitting next to their cardboard box sleeping quarters under a bridge underpass.

I felt sorry for them so I gave one a quarter cause he had asked for one so he could get a cup of coffee to warm up. After giving him a quarter he stumbled to the nearest bar. I checked the bar later to find that they never serve coffee. One day I saw a person give a pan handler some money so I watched him go around the corner and climb into his new Lincoln Continental.

CHAPTER 22

MORE PRECIOUS MOMENTS

Who put that manure spreader on top of that barn?

Now I wonder who would do something like that? Somebody, maybe Oogy, Eyeballs or me? Willie wasn't in on this one. Anyway we had to have some fun and it was one heck of a project putting that spreader on top of that barn, I guess it wasn't meant to be there cause do you see the dent in the roof? Ain't that what Halloween nights are for? We thought so. You ought to see that outdoor toilet that's laying upside down. It's a real mess. Kids, Don't Try This At Home!!

I believe Jimmy H. was along that Halloween night when some of us guys put a farmer's manure spreader on top of his barn roof. We had a hard time getting that up there. Apparently they had a harder time getting it down cause it was still there a week later. We could see it from the school bus on the way home.

CHAPTER 23

WEINER DOG

Can you imagine somebody putting a wiener hotdog on one of our school buddies car shifting lever one night? It fit just perfect cause he, Leroy, didn't have a knob on the shifter lever. He had a knob there now and it looked good there, like something out of this world. He got in a little trouble cause the Mr. Policeman (old Sam that didn't have a car, no club, not even a uniform, remember?) had heard about the wiener robbery from the smoke house in the town meat market. The 4 of us, Oogy, Eyeballs, Willie and yours truly were very interrogated for the next 3 or 4 days. I don't know why but they always picked on us devils, me too. Willie was innocent on this one. I pleaded the 5th. . I plead the 5th amendment, not a fifth of booze. The others did too cause they weren't about to squeal on each other.

One other Halloween night during high school years a couple guys I know (let's call them No Name 1 and No Name 2) crawled into the girls Home economics room window that just happened to be unlocked, and proceeded to indulge in orange soda pop and cake from the Home Economic refrigerator. One of the guys grabbed a fire hose and hung it over the balcony above the gym and turned on the water. You never saw 2 guys run so fast to get the heck out of there and get out of town. Nobody else ever knew, and I ain't tellin' on myself.

We played the game of chicken quite often. Chicken was when racing side by side down the highway at night with the car lights off. The first to turn on his or her lights was chicken. I never lost. Kids, *please don't try this at home or any place else!!*

In those days drivers license seemed to be secondary in the country. One of our neighbor ladies didn't get her license until she was about 35 years old. One of my school buddies went to take his driver's test one day. The next morning I asked him how he did. He said he didn't pass so he got back in his car and drove back home. That was Jimmy.

CHAPTER 24

CARS and TOYS IN MY LIFE

If you don't want to hear about my cars and toys please proceed to the next chapter. I had several good old cars in my life time. We know about hind-site and for-site but I shoulda' kept them all. Shoulda', coulda', woulda' if I had room to store them. I coulda' had a car museum by now. And maybe it woulda' been profitable now. And like I say- my dream car is a 1959 Ford Retractable Hard Top. I'm still dreaming. And time goes on.

Fords aren't supposed to break down, they generally just need Fixing-or Repairing- Daily. I believe that's still better than the Shove-It or Leave It Chevy.

The first car I drove was Dad's 1929 Graham-Paige. It was a large, heavy 4-door inline 6 cylinder 110 horse power. It was really peppy cause it was hard to get 19 inch tires then so Dad had the local blacksmith guy (Dad really kept that blacksmith guy busy) cut the wood spoked wheels down to 16 " rims cause 16 inch tires were easy to get. It geared it down so top speed was 65 MPH even though Dad said it went 40 MPH.

With the 4 speed trany us kids could plow with it. And we did plow. We hooked onto the 2 bottom plow one day and cruised across the field about 20 MPH or so and lowered the plow into the ground. Man, did the dirt fly or what? All of a sudden something happened, if you may know by now, the plow hooked a very big, big rock and sprang that plow all to heck. I had a hard time explaining that one cause I didn't think Dad would believe that this rock also just popped out of the ground and jumped up in front of me.

Anyway maybe Dad figured the Graham was hazardous to us kid's health so he called the local junk man (that was junk-man Skinny) to come and get it. Old Skinny flipped that car over upside down, hooked on to it and drug it to town. If you ever heard a half-grown kid cry--that was me.

Then Dad got what he thought was a "real car". It was a '41 Chevrolet. I called it a "shove it or leave it". That didn't last very long after I put the pedal to the metal. Dad always told me don't drive this car over 50 MPH. He didn't say why or why not so I gave it a test drive, my style test drive. Dad never said how fast it would go but I could of told him that it would go 95 MPH and that was on a bad day. I found out later on that the engine had babbited rod bearings and they were not worth a darn (that's putting it mild). Dad new why it shouldn't be driven over 50 but "Some People's Kids do the Darndest Things". That's me and I did it.

The 2nd car in my life was the '37 Packard I mentioned. I traded it in on a '46 dodge at Uselman's Implement in Wadena after it blew that rod bearing. I needed wheels ASAP. You know how that is. Anyway the Dodge had fluid drive semi-automatic trany, a real luxury. Now I had the world by the tail again.

I gave Dad's '40 Plymouth coupe a test drive now and then. I thought I was good at test driving. Yah shuer!! One day a couple high school buddies (let's call them Willie and Chucky) and Chucky says "Does this thing have any brakes?" I don't know why he was so worried about brakes--I was only going 70 MPH. Anyway it had hydraulic brakes so I said "Yah it's got good brakes" so I pumped the peddle to the metal a few times, and a few more times and then pushed down hard. Well wonders never seize to amaze me cause to my surprise the left-front brake locked up tight, and I do mean tight. That old Mopar made an immediate left turn across the tar road and made a sudden stop on the opposite shoulder facing in the direction we just came from. I basically said" How about that"? Chuck said "Whew". And Willie? He was speechless for quite some time. I asked Willie how his underware was.

For some reason I got sick of the '46 Plymouth cause it would only go 95 MPH. Lead foot me wanted something faster so I bought a '53 Desoto with the Firedome V-8 engine and automatic trany. This baby was a mean machine to say the least. Once again I had the world by the tail.

Now dear Uncle Sam was calling so I volunteered for the draft. I let Ma use the Desoto while I was gone. That was a mistake cause Ma never changed oil in it and stuff. She just drove, drove, drove and drove. Man could she drive--all of about 20 MPH in town and it was mostly town driving. It was all carboned and sludged up and when I got home it couldn't take the shock of being driven normal. The engine got noisy, very noisy. It got worse and then really worse and I then realized a rod bearing was out, I mean caput. After looking at the crank shaft journal it was like beyond anything imaginable. There as about a ¼ " space between the crankshaft and what was left of the connecting rod, just about enough space for a piece of harness leather.

Well after some brainstorming I found an old piece of harness leather, precision carved it and put it in place. Believe it or don't believe it-- but that held up for quite a while in city driving. I thought I'd give it a real test drive on the highway. Mistake, bad mistake, bad deal. Well I needed wheels so you know what? I traded it off for a '59 Ford 352 cid engine Police Interceptor with straight stick trany and overdrive. Man this was a mean machine and could it go. My other half and a favorite cousin of mine can attest that it would cruise at 140 MPH and was still gaining speed. *PLEASE DO NOT TRY THIS AT HOME!*

I never was a real racing type guy myself. Never took it to the strip or anything cause it could be hazardous to people's health. I could get rubber in 2nd gear at 110 MPH, if that tells you anything. Now this buddy Tom couldn't stand it that I had a '59 Ford so he got one too. It was a nicer color and stuff but couldn't keep with me on a drag so I would let him start in low gear and me in 2nd gear. I still left him if the dust or in the pavement particles? Man did he get huffy and said "what the heck you got under that hood? I tore out the overdrive gear one time and bent over pushrods and valve stems several times just being a lead-foot. I tore the top manifold off so many times I could do it in the dark.

The engine had hydraulic lifters. That was bad deal. The lifters couldn't keep up with rest of the engine. I decided to put in heavy duty valve springs but we found out it already had double springs in it that tested ok. The exhaust valves were so big they almost touched the intake valves. So I couldn't hop it up anymore and maybe a good thing cause it already was hazardous to my health.

The '57 Pontiacs were generally the hottest machine at the State Fair Labor day races then. A buddy had a '57 and he couldn't beat me. He was a sore loser too.

Anyway I decided to trade it off for something reliable so made a move, an upgrade, downgrade, sideways, lateral movement or whatever to a (hold your breath now) a 1961 Rambler wagon. Don't ask me why, I don't know. The only good thing about it was the wagon part. The seat backs could be laid down to make a bed, and man was that handy, and bad news two!

The engine had an aluminum block with a cast iron head. It doesn't take a rocket scientist to figure it out that it ain't going to work. Went thru 2 engine heads and traded it off when the 3 rd one cracked. It had a goofy rear end on it too. We came home early one morning, after the night before, and someone (I guess that was me) hit a curb and punctured a front tire. I didn't feel like changing it so ran it till it came off the rim. Well the rim soon got sort'a square and real bumpy and choppy and noisy down the street. The neighbor's lights came on at 3:00 in the morning. Later that morning after the night before, I was to change the tire and wheel but it wouldn't fit. After much scratching my head I took it to the dealer where I bought it. They put the wheel on the back end and it fit. Well they of course thought I was out the night before. Anyway after they tried it on the front end, it would not fit. Man what a relief--- I didn't feel so bad then even though I did have a hangover. They determined the car had a wrong rear end part and the spare wheel only fit that.

Next-- if my memory serves me right (I know that's scary) my next set of wheels as '65 Dodge Coronet 440. 440 was the body style not the engine size. Nice but it was hazardous to my health too. One winter we had a lot of snow so I put 825x 15 inch studded tires oversized tires on the back for added traction. I got stuck one morning, a morning after a night before again?, anyway with speed shifting front and reverse I got out of the driveway but not without leaving some 3 inch deep grooves in the tar street about 12 feet long. Amazing thing about those studded tires. About 2 years later they outlawed studded tire in Minn. Minn was the abbreviation for Minnesota then. I sure do miss those tires.

Anyway the Dodge held up fairly well for me until one winter there was a Christmas Party I attended while working full time and building a house on weekends and nights. I needed to go to that party like I needed a hole in the head. But I went there, did that and I remember leaving the party and just below the little hill were these 2 guard rails, one on each side of the road? Well, believe it or not I managed to clobber both of them. That really woke me up.

Anyway I ended up in 3 feet of snow about 100 feet off the road. Guess I was knocked out for about 20 minutes cause all of a sudden sirens were blasting and lights were flashing in my face. For some reason the car trunk had popped open and a 50 lb box of nails were scattered over about 200 feet up the road. Mr. policemen called a magnet truck to pick up the nails. They brought the nails to me a year later. Now due to all this confusion and delay I was late for another Christmas Party which needless to say I needed like another hole in the head. Well the authorities wouldn't let me drive my car that night so I missed the second party. Maybe a good thing, very good thing. Sometime during the next foggy day the neighbors looked funny at me when I drove down the street. The left front wheel pointed way out and bent, the right front wheel pointed way out the opposite way and bent and one head light pointed up as if I were looking for airplanes or something. The front end shook, rattled and vibrated unbelievable, otherwise everything else was ok except my head which had a big bulge that started to hurt a little. A gallon can of oysters had popped open and was all mixed with broken safety glass on the back floor. We strained the glass out ok and fixed oyster stew the next day. End of the '65 Dodge. It's gone now. I remember.

Had another Mopar wagon later but it was a dog. Had a '63 Buick Riviera for a while until it blew up one morning. That was one of those mornings after the night before.

A '65 Mopar was the wife's beater. A '57 Fury II, the wife beat this one two. A '52 Ford pickup, a '60 Ford pickup, a '76 Ford pickup, a '68

Dodge Van (junk), an '80 Chevette. The '52 Ford pickup was my beater. One time wifey, myself and a friend of ours (we called her "Sweet pea") jumped in and sweet pea grabbed the ignition key when moving and the ignition sprang out of the dash and truck stopped. So to get even with her I grabbed her nylon. Most of it came off. We all laughed about that. We were on the way to a bar, joint, club for a couple drinks, as if we really needed more. Anyway I ordered a Harvey Wallbanger, sweet pea ordered an Elmer Fud Pucker, at least that's what she intended to say. Well Fud Pucker words didn't come out of her mouth exactly that way and we were asked to leave. Anyway we had Been there. Did that. I told them we have been kicked out of better places than that.

If you don't care for a Harvey or an Elmer how about a Norwegian Car Boomerang drink? One of those will go a long way.

That nylon was a great conversation piece hanging on my truck's side mirror. Two years later buddy Bob bought that '52 Ford truck from me with the nylon still on the mirror. He had a little rough time explaining that to his other half.

Before things get busy here Sweet Pea grabbed my tie one night about 25 years later (yah we were having a few but they weren't Harvey Wallbangers or Elmer Fudpuckers), anyway she said " that's getting even for my nylon you took from me 25 years ago one morning after the night before". All I could say was " I want to see that tie flying high on your car antenna until it rots".

The other cars I had have no real exiting memories. Thank goodness. Been there. Did that. I remember.

And speaking of our dear friend, "Sweetpea" had the radiator taken out of her big Dodge wagon and was having it repaired. I guess she was late for a Elmer Fudpucker party so she asked the radiator man if she needed a radiator in the car in order to drive it to the local party. UFFDA!!

Another dear friend (let's call her "Little M") came walking to our house one day and I asked her "why are you walking instead of driving"?. Little M replied "my car is down the street about a block and something is dragging under my car and making a lot of noise so I stopped". I said "it's not a person I hope". "No it sounds kinda' tinny".

The first thing that came to my mind was that Little M had lost the drive shaft and it was dragging. Anyway I went to her car and guess what was dragging? Yah, you are right, it was her car's gas tank. She said " is that anything serious"?

I told another lady one time that her muffler belt was slipping and she should get that fixed soon. I guess when she told her husband that he couldn't believe that she fell for that one.

CHAPTER 25

A TAIWAN EXPERIENCE

In Taiwan ROC I was working for a well-knowing US Inspection Company. They paid all expenses and hauled us to the job site with a bus driven by the locals. They drive on the right side of the road, more or less, but they have no speed limit in villages or anywhere. They just honk the horn and people scatter or else-- just like that. The foremen mentioned to the driver on the way home from the job to stop at a certain place (a bar) cause the company as throwing a party. OH, Man, just what I needed. Another party, another mistake.

The party started with everybody lining up against the wall. I was about 15th down the line when I noticed that the boss handed the first guy a bottle of beer. It was not just an ordinary bottle but a full quart bottle of rot-gut beer. He was told to guzzle it down without stopping or be called a chicken. Ok, he did. Next guy the same. By now I realized they were working their way down the line and would be coming down to me and eventually I would have to guzzled one down or else--. They guarded the doors, no way to escape so I figured I 'd just call Ralph right away. You know what I mean? Anyway the guy next to me just let the booze run down without swallowing. I had to swallow and much to my own surprise I woofed it down without barffing or calling Ralph as we say. Now everybody sat down. That was good cause I was about to fall down real soon. We ate at a rotating table full of fixin's like eel, octopus, black chicken, and all those scrumptious goodies. Sure was glad when that day was over. I did call Ralph once but think it was due to the slimy squid instead of the quart of warm beer. Wouldn't you think so?

CHAPTER 26

MY HORSE TRIGGER—

After high school I worked for a poor farmer called Johny one summer cause I had nothing else to do?? The room and board was good. After the fall harvest was done Johny didn't have any money to pay me but asked if I would take the Indian Paint gilding that I got attached to for pay. I did and now I had the world by the tail until a year later Trigger got lame in one back leg and someone offered to buy him from me. They talked me into it (vulnerable me) and I found later that they may have been horse thieves, crooks, real crooks that gave a shot into Trigger's leg that temporarily made him lame.

Johny was a continuous smoker. He smoked like a chimney. I never smoked wacky tobacco or anything similar but I sure did smoke legal cigarettes like a chimney too. I could out-smoke any chimney and I did. I didn't do it till after high school and that was corn silk we put in corn cob pipes that we had made. Cousin Don and Billy came up to the farm from the big city and we would go out in the corn field and make corn cob pipes, load it with dried silk so firm and fully packed and puff away. *KIDS Please do not try this at home*. That's the same cousin Don that measured the wieners at the Minnesota State Fair to see if they were 12 inches long. That's the same cousin Don that drank so much grape pop soda that he nearly got drunk from it. That's the same cousin Don that wouldn't drink cow's milk when he came from the big city to the farm--he wanted store milk, not cow's milk. Poor kid. Later I really started smoking so much that I would get up in middle of the night and puff down 2 or 3 Viceroy cigarettes in a row and go back to sleep. I quite Viceroys after someone told me that the filters were made of fiberglass. I needed that like a hole in the head. I'd be smoking while eating and now get a hold of this--I'd have one burning in the ashtray, one in my mouth and lighting another at the same time. Some people smoked 4 butts before noon. I smoked 4 before I got out of bed. That's not good.

Anyway I finally said to myself "self, I got'a quit". I did quit when I decided to go back to school at 49 years young. Cousin Billy was my age. He didn't quit. He's gone now .

CHAPTER 27

HDTV--

And now they got this new fang-dangled gadget called HDTV. I thought it stood for Heavy Duty Television until someone straightened me out and told me they thought it stood for Hi-Density-Television. Never was a gadget junky except for a cell phone. Heck I still use 3 ¼ " floppy drive disks in my computer. Over? I think I'm right with the program cause a few drinks ago a company I worked for was still using 5-1/2 inch computer disks. I tried to talk them into donating those computers to the "Computer Historical Society", if there was such an organization. Maybe I should start a Museum society like that and include the reel-to-reel automated UT tape machine system they used . Now that would be progress. My buddy asked if I was born in the basement and never brought up. Smarty. I could write a book about that guy.

CHAPTER 28

GUMBO, BOOYA and CRAWDADS!!

There are two kinds of gumbo--one kind you can eat and there ain't nothing better, the other is gumbo dirt-mud, N.D. mud, red clay, sticky red clay, and sticky gray clay and we'll get to that a little later on.

Booya is a Midwest (sometimes we're call Northern Great plains people) stew type soup made from everything from soup to nuts like pork, beef, turkey, chicken, turtle, veggies and stuff and maybe mountain oysters in a large cast iron kettle. Most Fire Departments have a Booya event every summer or fall. It's good stuff. If you haven't had it, you just need to try it.

Now the southern version is called gumbo. They put in chicken, turkey, pork, beef, alligator, turtle, shrimp, okra, and file' seasoning (that's Cajun stuff) good and good for you. Maybe you think I'm Cajun or am from the south by the way I talk but guess it just rubbed off cause I spent a lot of time down there.

Crawdads is another name for crawfish. Some southern folks suck the crawfish heads after they pull it off, still good and hot. Me? No way. I don't suck the heads but love that crawfish and Rock Lobster. At a joint (a joint is a bar establishment) in Florida I ate 110 rock lobsters one time to win a bet. Len said "let's go eat some Rock Lobsters tonight". I said "OK and losser buys". I didn't lose again. Alligator is OK in my opinion but tough as harness leather. I've Been there. Did that. I remember.

CHAPTER 29

CASTLE BURGERS and more BUFFETS

There I sat all broken-hearted---ate 25 burgers before Wayne got started. Wayne said "let's go to White Castle® and looser buys". That's when the burgers cost 9 cents. I had to eat 25 burgers to beat him. That'l learn 'em.

I love buffets. The best buffet I ever had was s Chinese buffet in Phoenix, AZ. A little young waitress patted my slightly protruding belly and remarked "baby?" I nearly fell over and probably would have if there would have been more space between the table and my belly. The four of us were in awe. Now would you believe she came over and did it the second time? No lie. Well anyway, she was sorta' right. Remember I'm all belly and no hips? Anyway she was, young and innocent and well deserving of the generous tip I gave her. Bro Les had a laugh of his life!

One of my grand Rug rats (I'll call him "Just") was traveling with us and we stayed at a motel across from a Chinese buffet joint. I ordered a half a buffet telling the waitress that I intend to eat only half of what I normally do. No sense of humor so that didn't work and they charged me full $$.

Anyway this young kid Just, a growing young boy and I've been there myself, proceeded to fill a plate once, twice, three times as I did too like there was a contest going on. Now I was full up to my ears and Just started packing down lettuce like it was the last lettuce on earth. He claimed that lettuce would pack his food down so he could cat more. I think it worked. It was working for him. Finally after 2 hours Just had enough. By this time the Manager was getting a kick out of it so he asked Just if there was anything else he could get him. Just said "yah, you can get a wheel barrow and haul me across the street to the motel".

Two years later I stopped at that Chinese buffet place again and the Manager asked "where is my buffet eating buddy?" He remembered.

Here back home I discovered a way to keep food costs down when we invite friends and relatives over for supper. Supper, that's the meal we have in the evening that some people call dinner. I tell them ahead of time what I am making . It worked real well especially when I told them we would be having skin-on Norwegian meatballs and deep-fried mountain oysters or the all-time favorite barbecued beef brains with sauerkraut. I'm thinkin' my next book should be called "Norwegian of Minnesota Cook Book".

I've Been there. Did that. I remember the southern states of Texas, Louisiana, Mississippi, Georgia, Florida, and Alabama. Enjoyed the people and the good food in all of them. The best thing I liked about Texas was their Mesquite Bar-B-Q and their state income tax. They don't have any State Income Tax. The worst is their temperature--they have 2 temperatures there-- hot and hotter. It's typically 110 F in the shade and usually no shade with 95 % humidity in the summer with summer lasting most of the year. One thing I liked about Houston, TX was plenty of old cars available. I bought a few 1959 Fords that are waiting for me to get off my butt and restore. I feel they may be waiting a little longer.

I guess you could say I'm a '59 Ford buff with the big Fords and several toy Ford cars, '57's, 58's, and '59's. My dream car is a 1959 Ford Hard top retractable. I'm still dreaming.

CHAPTER 30

NORTH DAKOTA GUMBO

This is the kind of Gumbo you should not eat if you can help it. There are two kinds of gumbo-one kind you can eat, the other kind is gumbo dirt-mud, N.D. mud, red clay, sticky red clay and sticky gray clay. Got stuck in gray clay in cousin Jr.'s drive way cause it was so sticky it stuck to the car tires until the tires got so big that they filled the wheel wells up so the wheels couldn't turn. That's gumbo. Had a heck of a time getting the stuff off the car bottom. Best wait till it dries-which could take days. Well I didn't have days time --it was our honeymoon. OH Yeah!!

And then one time in western N.D. was driving in a park area and the road got narrower and narrower. No signs or any clue that the road may be ending . Anyway the tar turned into dirt, red dirt. It was red dirt until it started raining. Well it wasn't red dirt, it as red clay, real sticky red clay gumbo. It rained pitchforks and hammer handles so more red dirt turned into more red clay. The tires got real big and then guess what--the road ended right there, against a fence, a barbwire fence with some beef cattle starring at us. Us was my mother and I and yah Ma said "think we need to turn around". Well that was easier said than done. Now I got really stuck. Lucky I had a wire cutter cause I cut barb wire from that ranchers fence and wrapped it around the back tires to serve as chains. It worked quite well. The moral of this true story is "don't go to North Dakota without tire chains". Been there. Did that. I remember.

Here is a list of reasons why I like North Dakota:
.1
.2
.3
.4
.5
Next Chapter

CHAPTER 31

HOW TIMES HAVE CHANGED

I remember back in the '40's when Dad said it cost $10,000 to raise a kid. That was when a pair of bib overalls cost $1.69. Yeah, bibs were the "in thing" then. A candy bar, a pack of gum, a cup of coffee or a soda was a nickel. And the candy bar was bigger than they are now. Gas was around 20 cents a gallon at a full service station. Yeah, all gas stations were full service then. They would pump your gas, check the engine oil, wash the windshield and check the wiper blades and tire pressure.

A bottle of beer was 15- 20 cents. (not to get side tracked but the first beer I ever had was a Grain Belt one fall during the harvest time and that was only a ½ a beer). Dad bought a case for the local threshing crew when they were at our farm doing the threshing. I was floored when he asked if I wanted one. I thought to myself, "self, how long do I have to say yes, "Yes".

Remember when inside plumbing was nonexistent in the rural areas? Even small towns had little houses in the back yard and they weren't fish houses. If you never had to do your chores in an out house at 40 degrees below zero let me tell you, you ain't missing nothing. On the farm we had Montgomery Wards catalogs instead of toilet paper. Not real good stuff. And now days kids think they have it rough? They ain't seen nothin' yet.

Something else changed since I was a kid, like eating. When I grew upon the farm the meal at noon was called dinner, and the meal in the evening was called supper. Now they call supper, dinner and noon dinner as lunch. Well heck I have lunch between breakfast and noon, between noon and evening and sometimes before bed. Do you suppose that's why I'm all belly and no hips?

CHAPTER 32

DADS AND MOMS DO CRY

I could see the pain. I could see the tears in their eyes when they said "we don't have money to send you to college".

I mentioned before that the First Great Depression lasted through '39 or more like '42? It seemed more like 1942 cause I remember when Dad didn't or couldn't have modern farm machinery like a manure spreader or a tractor. Heck we barely had a barn for the milk cows and the milk cows were important. Remember the barn without gutters? Remember that barn with a straw roof? Well, the cows were lined up in a row and neatly tied up so they couldn't go outside to do their "stuff". But we had to help Dad clean up that "stuff" and haul it out into the fields. It was fun in the winter when us kids would tie our homemade sleds behind the manure wagon and slide along with Dad. Dad made sleds for us. He made wooden skis for us out of ash trees after he would saw the lumber from a tree, soak it in water several days or weeks and then tie the lumber in the rafter of the shed and pull it so it was bent to form the front end. Dad had imagination to no end.

In those days it was normal to have 2, 3, 4 feet deep snow so the horses almost got stuck. Those were the days when the temperature was normally minus 20, 30, 40 degrees below zero (that's a minus 40 degrees F). But some people today say we don't have global warming. I believe it is more than just Minnesota warming. I won't get into that now, it gets political and I don't want to touch it with an 11 foot pole.

CHAPTER 33

KRABBY KRAFT CAR PARTS

Krabby Kraft was the handle many friends put on Frank. Allow me to refer to him as "instigator vodka drinking Frank" but of course I always went along with his shenanigans. Anyway Frank was of German decent and I worked with him doing water well drilling before both of us figured it out that it was a dog's life. He is the buddy that fixed Mr. policemen's flat tire on his squad car and got me off the hook. I mean off from getting the book throwed at me.

You see, Frank and I were racing and it was not on a race track. If you ever heard 2 screaming cars at night in town going thru stop signs and over railroad tracks sideways, well that was Frank and me on the way to Frank's place after the bar closed? Yah we had a few drinks again and we threw away the caps and the corks from the vodka and Windsor bottles again. Frank snuck in with 1 quart of vodka, and me, I dragged in my usual 1quart of Windsor with the trimmings.

I may have mentioned this before, anyway this was the race that I beat him to his service station that he owned and operated and the Mr. policeman followed right behind. He didn't like the idea that I passed Frank 50 MPH sideways over the railroad tracks in town. No sense of humor. I fumbled to find my drivers license but dug out a Saint Christopher's medal my wife had given me and I said "Mr. osifer, I mean officer, will this do instead?"He had us both in his car cause he maybe figured both of us were 3 sheets to the wind. Anyway buddy Frank got out of the police car and took a walk. He came back in about 5 minutes and said to the policeman "are you going to let him go free?" When the policeman said no Frank said " do you want that flat tire on your car fixed, or not"? Because Frank owned the station that we were parked in front of he had the tools and air all handy.

Mr. Policeman looked out, saw that he had a flat tire and responded "Damm, OK fix it and forget about all the charges." He tore up the paper work he had started and dropped all potential charges on me. What a break for me. I was so happy I could of almost kissed him any place he would of wanted.

Anyway the next day I picked grass and gravel out of the tire beads and rims on my car. I had a headache, Frank had a headache too so we came to a conclusion that we should reduce our bottle sizes and not throw the caps away next time.

Krabby Kraft and I had too many vodkas another time (one night before the morning after) we both "called Ralph" on the front steps, side by side, on Assumption church at the same time. Frank was driving sorta' (swaying back and forth across the road but driving) and all of a sudden I said "Whoa, I got to call somebody". I meant I needed to call Ralph of course. ***Kids, please don't do this at church.***

And we had more good hazardous times too numerous to mention. Frank smoked cigarettes like a chimney. I'm sorry to say "he's gone now".

Uncle C lived to be 100 years old. Us kids asked him what he attributed his longevity to. He simply replied "I stayed single and drank every day, not booze but mucilage".

CHAPTER 34

UNCLE SAM CALLING

Back when they had the military draft Uncle Sam, the US government, would send a letter to young men that said "Greetings, We Want You". It really meant you were to report and get abducted into the armed services. They would pretty much decide which branch to put you in. Anyway shortly after the Korean Conflict (Korean War) truce, meeting, it didn't take rocket scientist to see that my number was coming up real soon to be drafted. Well I beat them to it. I went to the local draft board and volunteered for the draft to get it over with so I could get on with my life without interruptions. You see, I knew a girl that I wanted to spend my life with so--I guess you know the rest. One good thing with all this was that I would come back to the packing plant where I worked with all seniority. No if, ands or buts.

Three high school class buddies volunteered at the same time -- Eyeballs, Willie and Oogy. Here I was, a farm boy now down in the big city and they were up in the north woods country located at different draft boards. Anyway we all got together in Fort Chaffee during the 1st 6 weeks basic training. It was Party time again and I almost missed revile in the morning. That could of been a bad deal, real bad deal. "Oh boy".

Basic training--that's where they had everyone hurry up and wait-- wait in line for the first army haircut (yes we were in the army now).They cut every body's hair the same, real short. Of course they would ask how you want it cut. Some guys fell for it saying " leave the sideburns, and give me a light trim." Guess what? That barber took a big electric shears and made a path right up thru the middle, over the top and down the back. "Oops Sonny". One recruit messed up in formation and the Sergeant asked him "How long have you been in this man's army"? He replied "all day Sir".

Anyway revile was at 5:00 AM and we made it ok. That's when they blow a horn that sounds like taps. Then you manage to walk or limp, get into formation and stand at attention if you can motivate that far in the morning after the night before.

One week passed and the first pay day came. It was a whopping $20 advance payment. With that money we had to buy soap, wash cloth, tooth paste, tooth brush, and all other necessities, 2 of each, one for inspections display and one to use. My inspection stuff collected dust so maybe that was why I never advanced beyond rank of PFC.

In the 2nd 6 weeks basic training I volunteered for survey school. Surveying must have been important in Korea cause guess where they sent me? They sent me to Korea, the land of sliding doors and ____-____-___'s.

My buddies got to go to Germany. Where did I go wrong? What a deal that was. Anyway I was headed for Korea after 31 days of revile and rain and hurry up and waiting at the west coast. They ran us onto a Navy ship as if we were a herd of cattle and the ship headed for sea.

Now, I always was a real barffer when it came to riding in a car backwards and stuff and this ride was no different. On the 3rd day a storm comes up like none other and the air sickness or sea sickness, you name it, attacked me right now. Stuff from the medics didn't even help. The only food that staying down was soda crackers. To add to the misery, they had me on guard duty, 4 hrs on, then 4 hrs off, then 4 hrs on and so forth. Me not being a complainer just took it with a stride. Anyway, apparently the stairways on the ship had wings or something cause we had to guard a stairway, an empty stairway, nobody ever used it but just needed to guard it anyway. Oh well, it all paid the same.

Being sick and all this, I wanted off guard duty so I discovered a rash on my ankle and the medic got me off guard duty.

Anyway after 17 days on water we docked at South Korea. When we stepped on the ground it felt wavy and I thought it was a swamp. It felt like that for 2 or 3 days. If you Been there. Did that. You would know what I mean.

So they piled us in a duce and a half and gave us a scenic tour past the city of Soul and up to the DMZ. The DMZ, that's the place where it's too close for comfort. The cook in the company was actually a mechanic and he didn't like cooking so I need not say any more about the burnt food.

I used my survey skills there shooting some mountain tops for elevation like Pork chop Ridge. It was hard to climb Pork Chop without enemy shooting down at us. I can't imagine trying to climb it in war time with North Korean Joe shooting down on us. God Bless Our Soldiers.

The Korean people were poor then. Most lived in clay and grass huts with a stone floor that was warmed by a fire under the floor. There weren't many trees left anymore so twigs and brush was their fire wood for heat and cooking. Speaking of cooking--more than once I witnessed the people cooking a dog over a fire on the ground, fur and all, head and all, legs and all, a complete dog. You see, beef was sacred to most of them, it was their work animal, and I respect that. I got boozed up one time, or two times and ate dog meat without knowing it until after. It sorta' tasted like regular pork, sorta'. And mixing it with Korean booze that tasted like gasoline was a bad deal. Almost missed revile the next morning too. Guess you know what I mean if you've Been there. Did that. Remember?

G. I.'s were not supposed to go off-limits but almost everything and everyplace was off-limits. Everything off the shoulder of the main roads was off-limits. I was stationed in a Headquarters battery where officers and generals and us peons mingled together. Our department section was in charge of maintenance and stuff. I had to paint the 4-star general's recreation room. Yah he had rec room. Our rec room was the guard station. We had duty again nearly every other day and night. Anyway the general let me shoot pool on his private table. I didn't have to brown nose him either he was just an OK guy. Us guys drank beer, good beer, all export stuff, 12-16 % alcohol stuff and watched movies at the company Quonset hut movie house on base.

CHAPTER 35

EAT NOODLE SOUP WITH CHOP STICKS

When was the last time you ate noodle soup with chopsticks? Wisconsin Charlie and I went to Japan for a little R & R one time. The trip over was one-of-a-kind. We flew over there free on an old dilapidated two engine "flying boxcar" plane. That's the plane with the big belly underneath and only two prop engines. These planes were not able to fly on one engine according to the pilot. I believed him cause who was I to know any different. It was one hell of a ride on that plane. I almost called 'Ralph' more than once before we landed in Tokyo on one wheel with one engine smoking.

Anyway R & R stood for rest and recuperation. Some G I's called it I & I instead. I wonder what that meant?

We checked in at an Americanized Special Services Hotel for G I's just to be sure we had a backup place to hang out and eat reasonably. We ate some American food there until we got accustomed to the layout of the big city. One day we decided to try something different so we went to a Japanese restaurant. After sitting down and looking at the menu both Charlie and I discovered we had a problem. I couldn't read the menu, I couldn't speak or understand Japanese. Charlie was as dumb or dumber than I was. He just kept saying "me no comprendy". Charlie didn't realize he was trying to talk in Spanish instead of Korean. That didn't work real well. The waitress couldn't make heads or tails from those words either. The waitress couldn't speak or understand English. I thought she was dumb. Houston, we had a real problem.

I was really hungry by now so I put one hand over my eyes and pointed down on the menu with a finger from the other hand smack dab down on the menu. Charlie said "me samo, samo, I'll have the same". The waitress said some words that went way over my head and she just smiled and nodded her head up and down. Finally she returned with (get a load of this) 2 bowls of soupy noodle soup. One was for Charlie and I assumed the other one was for me? Yah, I guess that's what we had ordered, soupy noodle soup. Well I was hungry enough to eat almost anything by now including the hind quarter of a bear so I didn't complain. Now you may not believe this but I was looking for a spoon. Charlie was looking for a spoon. I looked again for a spoon. Charlie says to me "did you get a spoon?

I said "no".

Charlie said "we have a problem".

We tried to explain that we needed a spoon but the communications didn't register whatsoever. After more talks which none of us understood that waitress brought over a bowl of soup and motioned for us to watch her demonstration on how to eat soup with chopsticks. If I hadn't seen it with my own eyes I wouldn't of believed it. She got her head down sorta' close to the bowl, opened her mouth and started whipping those sticks like she was doing a drum roll. She started sucking harder and harder until a steam of juice started coming up, then some noodles came up. The more noise she made the more gross it was but it worked fine for her. Charlie looked at her. Charlie looked at me. I looked at her. I looked at Charlie. Both of us without saying another word grabbed our bowls, tipped them up and drank the soup down in about 10 seconds.

Ok, by now we had a few too many drinks that the waitress brought so we did get a taxi somehow so we could get out of this mess.

I told taxi "I, we want to go to G. I. Hotel. Do you know where it is?"

Taxi man: "yes, I take you there, no problem. Yah no problem."

Well taxis were cheap there but that ride cost me $30 USD cause I didn't know where he was going but I knew he wasn't going straight to the hotel. Later I found out that the hotel was only 2 blocks away from where I got the taxi. That learned me. I had to call home, collect, to have Dad send me some more money. I'm not real sure if Dad believed me about the taxi thing and why I needed more money, again, but I think he got over it. I think so. The way I look at it—Dad really maybe didn't understand everything cause he was never in the army, aside from being in Korea? Later on I told Dad "Well holy mackerel, if you ain't been there, you really don't know the whole deal". Yeah he got over it.

Anyway Charlie and I had a ball to say the least. We had planned to see all of Japan in 2 weeks time but there was so much to do and see in Tokyo that we had no reason to go further. Bar alley had it's good points—not sure what they were though. There were drinks, beer, wine, booze and probably women. I didn't get too involved with the last item. I heard tell that most girls there wanted to marry most G. I's and that was scary. What would I do with one of those? That's what my buddy said too "what would you do with one of those, you can't take her home with you on the ship". I said "buddy, I ain't going home on any darn ship".

Anyway finally my 16 month Korean tour, and Charlie's too, that lasted 16 ½ months, was over with and it was now time to go back to the states and get released on an early discharge. Well wouldn't you know us guys had a few beers at the movie house to celebrate another day gone by and that buddy of mine from Hurley, Wisconsin (the one we been calling Charlie) bet me that I would be going back to the states on a ship with him. I said "no I am going to fly instead". Charlie said "you did brown nose the General when you was painting the General's entertainment room and kitchen and hallway and bar, huh?" Anyway we ran out of the movie house with a beer or two or three in hand and I tried to take 6 steps down the hill at one time. That was a bad deal. Something went wrong and I fell to the ground. I had a big, big, big bulge on my ankle, big as a goose egg. My Hurley buddy Charlie and a heavy duty muscle man medic friend grabbed me and headed for the Medics. This medic friend said "thought you were going home tomorrow?" "Yes I am". "No I don't think so". Man that hit me like a lead balloon. My medic buddy said "they will more than likely fly you home to the states". I said "bye Charlie, I told you so".

Anyway I like to keep things short so to keep things short they put my right foot in a cast and flew me home air evacuation. On the way back to the states they stopped at Honolulu hospital for a couple days. The hospital was up on a hill. I could see the lights of town but they wouldn't let me out to go down and man that hurt worse than my leg did. Maybe they thought I would go A-Wall. Maybe they were correct.

Anyway they flew me and a bunch of other decripilated individuals to the Great Lakes Hospital in Chicago for ankle rehab which I figured would be about a couple days. Wrong. They would not let me out on the early discharge until I could walk without the slightest limp. I tried to fake a limpless walk but that didn't work. Before they let me free from the hospital they tried to get me to re-up for another 4 years in the man's army but I told them where they could go! And it wasn't to heaven.

Anyway I won that bet with Charlie. Charlie, if you are out there somewhere reading this – remember I told you so. Been there. Did that. I remember.

CHAPTER 36

BACK HOME

I got back home, went back to the packing plant, got back with that great girl I had known and got married. (all in that order). I won't elaborate any further about how and where. I plead the fifth.

My best man (let's call him Tom) that's my buddy who's girl friend Ern accidentally lost her engagement ring down the sink drain and here one day I saw Tom all sloppy and slimy digging up the septic tank and stuff in his Dad's yard. He was screening all the stuff with his Ma's spaghetti strainer looking for her ring. The words as I remember were something like this: (and some that I cannot mention here)

Ern: "Tom, my engagement ring went down the drain".

Tom: "Did you get it out"?

Ern: "No".

Tom: "Jeeeeeeese, for Christ's sake, were you born in the barn and never brought up—or what"?

Jee---eeeesese was one of Tom's famous words. He said it that time when we almost lost his boat down the Mississippi river that time. This was the same Tom that was with us the night we got caught in the city swimming pool after hours. Tom's the one that got caught borrowing lead pencils from the local Dime Store and told Mr. policemen that he needed them cause the teacher told him to write a book. Tom let us take his '56 Ford car on our honeymoon. Man could that Ford move? Tom is the guy that when some of us guys, me, Wayne and Les told him we had tipped his boat and lost it in the Mississippi river said " OH well". Then when we told him it was just a prank he got real mad and threw rocks at us. Tom was one of my buddies that had a Harley Davidson - like my bro Les and me. Tom was the guy who picked me up when I crashed my '49 Harley the last and final crash. Tom was the guy who quickly grabbed a hacksaw and helped saw off bro Les's back fender from his Harley Sportster when it reared up on the hill climb event and the fender buckled up under the frame. Willie, that's Les, won a trophy that day. I say Thanks to Tom for that.

Tom was the greatest of guys. He was a fun guy even though he was always letting off lima bean gas when we least expected it . He's gone now. Them darned tumors, I hate them.

Les was the one bro that shot bro Marv on the ear lobe with a Daisy air rifle or BB gun from the upstairs window. Les is the one that said "let's play follow the leader". Me dumb--I said "Ok". So Tom, Wayne and dumb me followed Les on our Harleys going 60 MPH in a 30 MPH zone down the center line with cars going both directions, and me watching Les's knuckles clicking on the car doors. That was once, me not dumb no more! Been there. Did that. I remember.

CHAPTER 37

THE MIDDLE-AGE SPREAD

And now the middle-age spread, also known as the tumor years, are approaching us. I'm all belly and no hips. It's not a beer belly, it's a food belly. It's a lack of sit-ups. Sit-ups at my age? Ouch!

My pants size varies depending if I wear suspenders or not. I need a size 6 sizes bigger when I wear the suspenders cause they hold the pants up where they should be, up there by the bulge, the inner tube. Suspenders keep my pants off the floor too. I got the short end of the deal when legs were passed out. Like I mentioned before my inseam is 28 inches maximum and that's on a good day. I know today's fashion is to let the pants hang down and walk on them and have the crotch at the knees but I prefer to take full-size steps, if the rest of my body will permit it.

Dad once said and I quote him, "it took me years to learn to say yelly and then they went and changed it to yam". Dad liked food too. He had to wear suspenders too, or walk on his pants. When things got better in the '50's Dad would eat like a horse. On Holiday get-to-gethers, usually for dinner and for supper, Dad and us boys always had a contest to see who could eat the most cause Ma would cook enough to feed an army. Dad usually won those contests. Kinda' crazy, wasn't it? No wonder we were poor. I remember one time Dad came home from a hunting day and said he got a goose for supper. Well, he had it in a bag and who were we not to believe him anyway. Ma cooked up that "goose" and man was it good? It was a big one but it was all gone within a half hour. All of a sudden Dad said "how did yous like that raccoon"?

Ma always said don't eat stuff like that, it will catch up with you some day. Well, Ma was right but she didn't say that Dad and I would be all belly and no hips some day. Anyway, I Love you Ma.

I guess Ma figured fruit would be good for all of us so she planted about 18 fruit trees of various nature such as peach, apple, cherry, plum, apricot, and some cross-bred fruit stuff. After 6-8 years they started bearing some nice eatable fruit. Ma had intended to can the fruit and make sauce, and jelly (or was it Jam?). Anyway there wasn't as much fruit left on the trees when she decided to can it as there was earlier in the season. Huh! Ma said " I wonder where all the fruit went"? She thought maybe the birds ate it all so she told Dad " do something about those dirty birds. Shoot them or something". I said " Oh Ma you can't do that".

So here is Ma, no fruit to can, no sauce, no jelly, no jam so of course she goes to town and buys a bunch of crates of fruit, peaches, apricots, cherries and cans all those. She made about 100 quarts of sauce or so. She made 30-40 pints of jelly, (or was it jam?) during the summer time so we had stuff for the winter. She would make pear and rhubarb and strawberry sauce too.

So of course winter came and one day Ma asked me to go in the basement and bring up a quart of sauce. I didn't want to go but didn't want Ma to suspect anything so I stumbled down the steps to the basement. I had one heck of a time telling Ma that there was no sauce in the basement.

I had a harder time explaining where all her 50 gallons of choke cherry wine disappeared too. She found out about the wine when she found the brown gallon jugs in the woods the next spring.

I ain't tellin' who ate the sauce but that sure was good wine. Would you believe somebody's kids went in to the basement and sneaked out a quart or two of sauce at a time and would take them in the woods and eat it, just gobble it up like it was the last on earth. SOME PEOPLE'S KIDS DO THE DARNDEST THINGS!!

I recently discovered a way to keep food costs down when we invite relatives over for supper. Supper, that's the meal we have in the evening that some people call dinner. I tell them ahead of time what I am making . It worked real well especially when I told them we would be having skin-on Norwegian meatballs or deep-fried mountain oysters or the all-time favorite barbecued beef brains with sauerkraut. I'm thinkin' my next book should be called the "Norwegian of Minnesota Cook Book".

I'll invent a fat-free blue cheese dressing or something similar. I asked the waitress for fat-free blue cheese dressing for my salad when I went to a restaurant. The last time I asked for it the waitress said "what planet are you from?"

CHAPTER 38

RETIREMENT TIME

Retirement? That's when a person quits work and quits making money for someone else and do nothing except lay on the couch. Right? No that's when a person quits working for someone else and does the things he's always wanted to before. I wanted to retire at 55, then at 65 but I had it all figured that I couldn't because I had so many things planned to do that I wouldn't have enough time so I continued to work. The legendary Swift & Co went belly up in South ST. Paul so my early retirement at 55 went out the window.

My last job traveling for the inspection company was to Philly again. I flew home and emailed the boss with these kind words "If there ever was a company and people I enjoyed working for -this was the one . For you I have climbed the highest tower, and crawled in the tightest spaces but he damn pneumonia got me down. This is my official announcement that I am going to retire November 10th at 5:00 PM. 2005. Don't call me, I'll call you. You all are welcome to come up to the house here in God's country but you may see a sign on the door--GONE FISHIN".

Anyway I made the brave movement to retirement at 69 years young. Don't know which project I'll start tomorrow. I could do yard work, fix the driveway, cut down the sumac brush that will be taking over the back yard, wash the windows, paint the wood windows before they rot and fall out, re-do the sagging mail box, plant some grass seed, knock down the bee nests under the house eve, rearrange the basement, (I mean basically clean it out), not to mention clean up some of my old toys after I find them, fix the rust on my truck, wash wife's car, and my trucks. How can I go to an auction with all this stuff staring at me? Ok. I got my priorities in order now.
Priority #1: antique auctions
Priority #2: restoring my 3- 1959 Fords
Priority #3: other projects

I Retired on November 10th, 2005 at 5:00 PM and haven't gone fishin' yet. Maybe cause I live on a river? Been there. Did that. I remember.

CHAPTER 39

REMEMBER WHEN

Remember when you could use a knob on the steering wheel of your car? It gave the driver good quick control when needed and was an excellent safety feature but they went and wrecked that.

Remember when you could say to Mr. policemen "sorry I didn't stop for that stop sign but I'll stop twice for the next one I see". And "Ok osifer, I mean officer, I didn't know you were there watching me and no I wasn't drinking much lately".

Remember when you didn't need to wear seat belts? Cars didn't have seat belts?

Remember when butcher knives were for butchering—like butchering a hog—a sow or a bore? Well bro Les and I discovered another useful purpose for a butcher knife. We were doing a remodel job on a favorite cousin's house (let's call him Dewey) when his wife was in the hospital having a baby. Dewey not liking to cook never refused to accept food donations from the neighbors. They brought over hot dishes and cold dishes and stuff. Dewey didn't have room in the frig and oven any more to store the food but he always told them "yah we could use some more". Anyway to make things simple, easy and less dishes to wash we hung a butcher knife over the middle of the table where the 3 of us could reach. We used it for everything like cutting, buttering bread and you name it, we did it. KIDS, DO NOT TRY THIS AT HOME!!

Remember when milk cost less than a dollar a gallon at the store? Milk is going up- the cows must be getting lazy or tired. Speaking of milk, cousin Don didn't want to drink cow's milk, he wanted store bought milk. Well, he had to settle for cow's milk when he was on our farm. That learned 'em.

Remember when a pair of farmer type bib overalls cost $1.89 at the local clothing store and there were no such thing as a discount store. There was no such thing as a dry cleaners in our little local town.

Indoor plumbing was actually in the outhouse, outside and unheated. Uff'da. A pile of Montgomery Ward catalogues was there for the mop-up. The price was right for the catalogues cause they sent them annually if we ordered something. MA always ordered something cheap from a couple different companies so we had a year's supply of those Montgomery Ward handy wipes.

Remember when shoes were worn only when we went to town or church or a wedding?
Remember when you used to do things all night and now it takes all night to do it? An example is: we used to could drink all night, get hammered, and now they call me the 2-beer kid.

Our friends Tom and Erna got married 3 times to each other and finally the judge said "you can't do that anymore". That learned 'em too. Not sure if I would marry the same woman 3 times if I had to dig up the septic tank to find her engagement ring that went down the septic system.

I remember this one guy who wouldn't eat fruit from the store unless he scrubbed it with a wire brush, soap and water. He said "can you imagine how many people have fumbled, played with and squeezed this fruit"?

Remember when you could hunt anywhere you wanted ? without any problems? It was a normal, natural thing to do. Neighbors were neighbors. That's what neighbors were for. Now you need permission and land owner's permits in some places.

Remember when there was no limit on squirrels? Anyway I don't think there was. If so, we didn't know or think about it. *As the world turns. No, I mean as the world changed.*

Remember when News Papers had news in them? Now I call them scandal sheets or soap opera papers. The first time I called them that at the news stand the girl almost had a hemraige.

It cost 9 cents to go to a movie at the local theatre.

The dentist didn't have Novocain to give when drilling a tooth.

The dentist did everything from cleaning to pulling teeth and everything between.

When you didn't have to take the keys out of the car ignition in town or at home.

When most houses in small towns didn't have indoor plumbing--heck they didn't have running water. I know water always runs down hill but you know what I mean? And you know what the plumber says about human waste? He says "It flows down hill".

When the previous year's Montgomery Wards catalogue was placed in the outhouse for the mop up, instead of toilet paper.

When farmers drove to town on the tractor cause they could burn tax-free gas in the tractor.

When Uncle Sam said "No, No you can't do that" if you got caught burning farm gas in the car. We had a plan to tell him that we use the Graham Paige like a tractor and that will only go 20 MPH. Man, was that a lie or what? Would I say that? Technically, I think any farm vehicle was not supposed to be driven over 20 MPH on the road. I told them, the Uncle Sam people that I consider this only a cart trail. They didn't go for that, either. Man it was tough trying to convince them any different.

Remember when gas was gas? Now what? Now they have regular unleaded, they have super unleaded, they have premium unleaded and you got to be real careful cause they have diesel. Some stations have a green hose thing for gas, some stations have a green hose thing for diesel. That could be an UFFDA!!

When there was no such thing as "pre-packaged food". Oopso, nil. Have-a no. We basically, sorta' lived off the land not only during the "Great depression" but after it too. I remember the tears in Ma's eyes when she couldn't give us kids that she wanted to.

The high school superintendent said that I had enough brains to go to college. You should of seen the tears in Ma's and Dad's eyes when they said "Son, we don't have enough money to send you to college".

When I banged up my ankle coming out of the bar in Korea that night, the night after the night before when we had a few 16 % alcohol beers, I didn't call Ma to tell her cause I didn't want her to worry. And I didn't call her when I was still laid up in the Army hospital state side for 2 months. Well, some people's kids do the darndest things! That was me, but not real prowd of myself for that. Kids, don't do what I did like that. Do right to your Ma.

When there was 16 oz in a lb of coffee and now you get a 13 oz lb.? Hey, I shouldn't weigh as much as I do. Right?

When people were born and died at home instead of in a hospital? If you don't date back that far allow me to explain the reasons why:
1. there was a shortage of the green stuff to pay the Doctor so he could check your blood pressure, and to pay the nurse so she could check your blood pressure, and to pay the hospital.
2. maybe the old modern "A" Ford wouldn't start.
3. maybe the team of horses were too wild that day to hook them up to the bobsled.
Been There! Did That! I remember!

I remember Dad telling about how the Grandpas and Grandmas got together, did their thing and brought me into this wild world? I remember when the Grandpas and Grandmas passed away and I got tears in my eyes as big as horse turds.

I was awake the night they carried Norway Grandma out from the back room of the 2 room house. (That was the house with a bed sheet stretched across the center to make a 2 room house.) Us kids were all boys then so I guess privacy wasn't so much a factor as existence was. The house was half dark cause we didn't have electricity.

I had those tears in my eyes when I saw Norway Grandma in that thing that looked like a big reed caned basket.

That Grandma stayed with us on the new 40 that Dad had bought in 1940. And you know what?—Norway Grandma was a sister to Grand Uncle Christ who showed Dad that 40 acres the day in 1940 when it was raining pitch forks and hammer handles. Grandma would sing to us and play with us 3 rug rats. She had a lot of long hair but not many teeth but she was MY Norway Grandma.

And I remember the old log house that Uncle Christ (from Norway) and the auntie lived in all their life. Us kids would walk over there a lot cause auntie made a lot of cookies and stuff. That old log house had 1 room downstairs and 2 rooms upstairs if I remember correctly. That's kinda' scary. I walked through that door many times. Been there. Did that. I remember.

They are both gone now and I have those horse-style tears in my eyes. The old log house is gone too but is still in my memories so here it is again:

Grand Uncle Christ's and Aunties log house. They too were true pioneers.

And then Grand Uncle Ole (from Norway) and wifie located in the Turtle Mountains of Nord-da-koda. Now get a handle on this ------- Ole was my Grand uncle, his wifie was another one of my Great Grandmas. Oh, this gets a little tricky. Anyway great grandma had some boys from her first marraige and one of the boys had some rug rats. That's where Ma came from. Anyway they too were true pioneers. Their log house is gone but the memories are still with me and I get those big horse style tears in my eyes when I see the only thing left on Great grandma's place is the hand well pump and root cellar. This is one of two things that remain of great grandma's place in the Turtle Mountains:

CHAPTER 40

IT'S LIKE THIS

GREAT GRANDMA'S WELL PUMP

This was taken "on the morning after the night before" (it was party time again) so I don't know if the pump was leaning or if yours truly was leaning.

You may have noticed that I treasure old stuff—the older the better. I cry when old buildings are torn down. They are history and cannot be replaced once they are gone. Anyway, Great Grandma on the Bottineau side –I loved her. I was her "Sonny". She always called me that. There isn't much left of her and Great uncle Ole's lakeside ranch. The old hand well pump and the root cellar in the hillside and a piece of the concrete slab where the front door used to be are all that's left.

Somebody has a garden in the same spot that Great Grandma had her garden. The bushes that were around the garden are now tall trees.

The barn was leaning toward the lake when I was a kid. Now it is gone and replaced with those new cabins down by the lake shore. But that was Great Grandma's place.

And cousin Curt, if you are reading this book, I thank you for preserving it. It is a legend in it's own right.

GREAT GRANDMA'S ROOT CELLAR

This picture was taken on a morning after the night before.

HAHN'S BAY STATE PARK

Anyway, one of Turtle Mountain great grandma's boys (my grandpa) , let's call him "Willie Hahn", and grandma married and located , in that order as I understand, on this spot at Lake Metigoshe. This picture was taken of Hahn's Bay by yours truly standing where their log house used to be. The log house is gone now. And I got tears in my eyes as big as horse turds.

When I was little I thought that everybody could die sometime but Bottineau grandma and grandpa could not.

CHAPTER 41

MORE THOUGHTS OF THE DAY

RIDING THE MILK COWS

Us kids had to walk ½ to ¾ mile to get the cows in the evening for milking. We would hop on a favorite cow, or bull and ride home to the barn. If the animal didn't like being ridden it would go close to the electric barb wire fence. They really weren't as dumb as they looked. Sometimes my toes got shocked each time they clicked on an electrified wire barb. It worked in their favor and that's when I picked up a club and the cow and I proceeded to have a meeting. and we didn't talk about the weather.

SOME PEOPLES KIDS

There are a couple in-laws that really love to paint, or getting even?. Anyway their father has a '57 Ford, 2-tone green, nice car, nice condition until one day the in-laws found some pink and white paint that they figured should be used before it got stale or something. Well pink and 2-tone green mix about as well as water and oil. At age 14 your guess may be better than mine. Anyway vendetta or what, they proceeded to paint their marks on their Dad's green car. There was no pattern, no reason, no rime but some people's kids do the darndest things.

Somebody's kids that I know put their little sister in the clothes dryer one time and turned it on dry cycle just for the fun of it. To the best of my knowledge she didn't get sick and call Ralph or anything like that. At least we didn't see any body fluids in the dryer tub. I guess that's where the expression "Vic is in the tub" came from? I don't have enough paper to continue that story.

AND TODAY

Mr. Itis is visiting again today. His first name is Arthur. He attacked my right foot. That's the one the John Deere tractor landed on when I was young, innocent, hard-up, broke, gutsy and stuff. That's the same right foot I sprained in Korea early one morning about 2:00AM after the night before, if you know what I mean. If Mr. Itis keeps attacking me I'll have to put my pants on sitting down instead of standing up.

AND TODAY I felt younger for a minute or two cause I was carded when buying some cigarettes. That made my day.

DRINKING COFFEE

When I was young and we went traveling one time my Dad saw a sign that said "CAFÉ". The Norwegian part showed up in Dad cause he pronounced it "coffee". Dad was a heavy coffee drinker and guess it rubbed off on me. I generally drink about 4-5 cups a day. My cups are Norwegian size cups which are equal to about 5 regular size measuring cup cups. Are you with me on that? So if 1 and 1 are still 2 as it was when I went to school, I slop down about 16 to 20 cups per day. Not too bad. Eh? Some times I say Eh cause I was born near Canada.

CLOTHING LABELS LIKE NONE OTHER

It has been determined that I was caught walking around with clothing store labels still attached. They called me Minnie Pearl but that didn't work although Minnie was one of my favorite Grand Ole' Opry entertainers. My other half reads clothing labels at Needless Markup retail stores and Dillie Bar stores.

THE F+ STUDENT, ALI HEMI

In 9th grade General Business class the teacher was a mean old thing (bless her soul) she would sooner whoop you as look at you. Anyway her thing was to take a test, then exchange papers around the class, correct the paper, and return the corrected paper to the proper owner. Then she would take roll call and the person would answer be telling his score for the test paper. Every time she called Ali he would answer "F+". He always had an F but wanted to make it sound a little better. After 2 or 3 years in the same grade I think they passed him to get rid of him. Bad deal that was. It didn't learn 'em.

HOW DO YOU SPELL "RELIEF"?

Answer: "TUMS". Or when your chins heal up and quit hurting after being kicked with spike heeled shoes.

Answer #2: When a woman's defensive spike heels and long nails no longer contact your body.

HOW COLD IS COLD?

Cold is when you have to light a bunch of corn cobs dipped in drain oil, light it afire and place it under the oil pan of the car to warm up the engine oil so the car will have a chance to start.

Cold is when you try to lick ice off a metal snow shovel and your tongue won't come off the metal in one piece. That's cold.

PET PEEVES

I DON'T KNOW WHY THEY (WHO ARE THEY?) call them pet peeves anyway. I don't see anything petty about them. I have a few that I want to mention and hope I'm not the only person that has some of these.

Here we go:

Those hard, clear plastic containers that cookies are packaged in that make a bunch of noise when trying to open them quietly cause I want to sneak a cookie.

Do you have a problem interpreting the Directories in some of these large malls? The way I see it they don't face in correlation to the North-South or even with the mall building.

Seat belts when I try to reach over to get something and the darn thing locks on me.

Automatic door locks on some cars when I wish they weren't locked.

Car and truck doors that won't open 90 degrees—you can't get big stuff into the cab. (who? Me?)

Pant legs that drag on the floor or even touch the heel of my shoe.

Itchy neck after getting a hair cut and 55 MPH speed limits

Sour milk—especially finding it out after I pour it on and taste my cereal

Muskmelon and limburger cheese, period.

Now hear this—if this won't peeve a guy off nothing will—you fill a shopping cart with groceries and get all checked out and find out they only accept debit cards and check cards (what ever check cards are) . No mention that those are the "only forms of acceptable payment".

Anyway I didn't have $220 cash on me at the time so we told them they could put their discount groceries where the sun doesn't shine. I guess a couple hundred dollars in sales didn't mean much to them. I got the impression they thought we were crooks or something. Well, that'll learn 'em.

I will have more pet peeves later. Guaranteed.

Here's another pet peeve of mine—
Wearing sunglasses

Wearing eye glasses (my eye doctor said I should wear sun glasses. It took a while to find exactly what I wanted but I bought some that are marked UV400) I wonder if he will approve of these!!

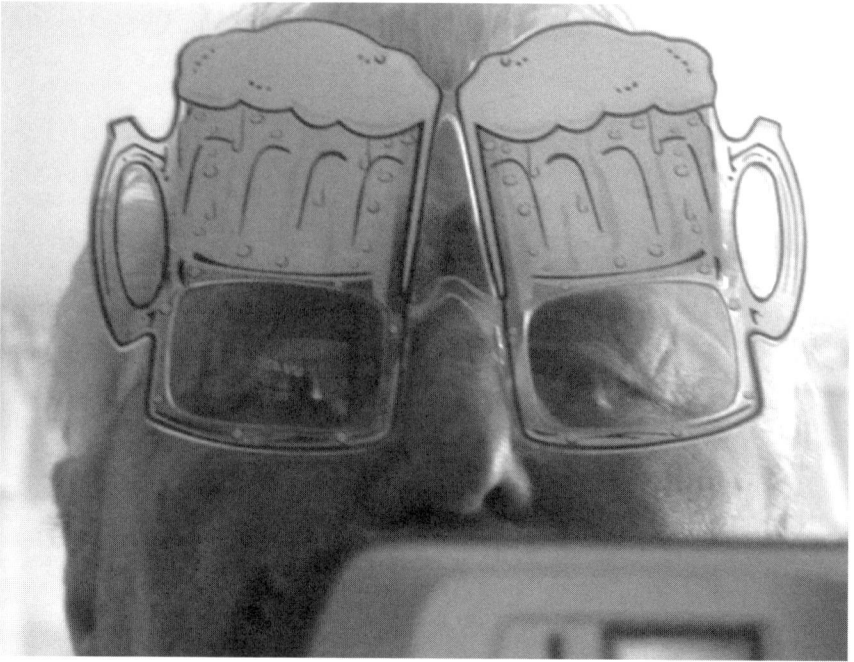

CALL ME THE 2 BEER KID

Call me anything but don't call me too late for supper. After more than 2 beers within a 10 minute time span I forget how to count and am not responsible for my actions especially before 8:00 PM. If you think that's bad, I'm not responsible for my actions with 2 beers after 8:00 PM. Sorta' scary?

I had more than 2 beers in a 10 minute time span that time the 2 guard rails jumped right up in front of my car. And I guess I had more than 2 Windsor and waters (or was it Harvey Wallbangers) the time I fell on the dance floor and Krabby Kraft Frank picked me up and proceeded to run cold water over my head stuffed in a small sink. Call me "sink banger", OK cause Frank said I was banging my head around all over the place. Remember Frank was the same guy that threw away the cap to his Vodka bottle at the dance. Good old days they were. Been there. Did that. I remember. The sad thing is: It will not happen again, guaranteed. That old well digger Frank is gone now.

One other night out at the local bar I learned a couple things. There was a heated discussion about DNA. One guy insisted that it stood for "DAH Normal Alcoholic" or "De Natural Alcohol". I wouldn't say much about the alcohol part cause I'm a 2 beer kid and am not responsible for my actions after 8:00 or after 2 beers, whichever comes first. My genes get fired up after 2 beers within 10 minutes time. My genes get a little jumpy after 2 beers after 8:00 at night.

Here I sit all broken-hearted, didleling with the stock markets, waiting to get started. I'm totally confused about the stock markets. One guys answer to that was "I must be paying attention anyway".

CHAPTER 42

REAL ESTATE

The wifie and I decided to go on a vacation one time. She wanted to go to Ireland. Of course I wanted to go to England so we compromised and went to Colorado. A couple times we went to the Dakotas and admired the Real estate.

I enjoy old architecture and old buildings so I have included pictures of some vacant buildings which I consider fortunate to have seen in the Great Plains and in the Dakotas. Some of them may be remnants of the 1930's "Dust Bowl" during the First Great Depression.

Since better days were here and I need to do something to keep occupied instead of becoming a couch potatoe I have thought about getting into Real Estate. I know a guy that buys and resells older "fixer-upper" type houses and buildings and comes out smelling like a rose. (That's what I need—to smell like a rose).

Anyway one of our trips through N.D. and S. D. proved interesting for Real Estate property. Some houses and stuff along the road caught my eye for some reason and I couldn't resist the temptation to click on them. These are pictures of some real Real-Estate along the way.

This is a nice fixer-upper home close to the road. One of those could be used as an outhouse.

This one has potential for outdoor plumbing.

There is potential here. This one has electricity outside.

Looks like this one needs a front door and maybe a piece of glass in a window but it has a fenced in yard and a storage shed.

How about a secluded location by the road in the trees for your private get-a-way?

Nice retirement farm located somewhere in North or South Dakota. The cars might go with the property if a person would beg real hard. It does need a little TLC.

This land comes complete with buildings, as is. Mineral rights are not included.

Heh! How about this one? It needs a couple windows but the chimney looks good from out here by the road.

OH YES!! Here we have a country farm house on nice slopping land with trees abounding. It's only about 99 miles from town.

As of today I have not placed an offer on any of these properties.

CHAPTER 43

THE MINNESOTA NUT TEST—
THINGS TO REMEMBER

Before I could work in a Nuke plant I had to pass a nut test, yeah that's what it was called, a nut test. I'm not knocking the test cause I believe in security of the highest degree. There were some real crazy questions in the test like this one comes to mind in particular—Do you ever see little hairy things in the toilet bowl? UFFDA! That one was easy. The test was engineered so that some questions were asked more than once just to see if they could catch a liar. I answered the above question the same both times. That was easy.

Speaking of nuts---I had a snowmobile one time. It was fun but hazardous to my health. Porkie was usually the leader of the pack except one time Sisco leaned on the gas after a couple Hi-Balls, or 2 or 3. Anyway he didn't see this one fence ahead and needless to say the top barb wire of the fence caught him right under the chin. Bad spot. Real bad deal. Anyway here we found Cisco laying in the snow bank a little bloody but still kicking. His snowmobile was still going full speed towards town as if it was trained to go to the local bar for a pit stop. We all needed another pit stop like we needed a hole in the head. Anyway Sisco got up, shook his head and took another swig of his strawberry wine. That learned 'em. He won't do that again. And now he's gone too.

Please get a hold of yourself before you fall over. I went horseback riding with a nutty guy who really was something. His name is withheld to protect the guilty. Let's call him "Something". Something said "get on that big horse and follow me ". Well I figured he was headed to the local bar for another Harvey Wallbanger drink or an Elmer Fudpucker drink. We needed that like hole in head. So I followed Something around the farm, through the woods, under some low tree branches and right into his trailer house. Yes, his trailer house. I mean to say the horse had no trouble stepping up the 3 steps into the house just like he belonged there and had been in it before. Anyway my horse was beyond control and when the 2 of them tried to meet in the narrow hall way unusual things happened. I mean real unusual.

They got stuck. Their big bellies pushed on the walls until they got untangled and we finally got out of there in one piece. Something had to do a little house cleaning after that juicy ride cause there was a pile of green, brownish fertilizer in the hallway that wasn't supposed to be there. The horses were relieved, literally. I was surprised that Something didn't leave the stuff there and try to grow a garden in it. He really was Something.

Wifie and I decided to take a vacation. We couldn't agree on Ireland or England so we compromised and flew to Colorado. Anyway up in the high altitude part a friend insisted we all go to the local Moose Lodge bar. We really needed that. Anyway I guess we closed up the bar place and much to my surprise we made it to the house in one piece and a few pounds lighter. I guess I called Ralph a few times. The next 2 days were rough because altitude and booze don't mix very well.

I remember the first time I sat down on a creeper, that's one of those creepy, rollercoaster, low profile, 4 wheeled thing-a-ma-jigs you can use to scoot around on the floor when working under a car. I tried to sit on one end and lay down, well the darn thing bobs up on the other end and hit me in the head. The next time it turned and flipped me into a pile of grease. I wasn't real popular after I put those clothes in the washing machine.

When I replace that clutch plate on the '37 Packard in the snow bank we didn't have a creeper. A sled worked better anyway. No I wasn't sliding down hill under the car, I was just sliding, period.

Speaking of cars again, My Grandmother told me that the greatest values in life was found in things we can't see, touch, or buy, like faith, love, family and 1959 FORD HARDTOP RETRACTIBLES.

CHAPTER 44

THE ORDER OF THE DAY

I usually wake up around 3-4 AM even if it is a morning after the night before. The night before means " out on the town and having a few beers" , or a few Harvey Wall Bangers, or at a dance at a set-up joint tipping up a few dozen Windsors and waters. Then do my usual morning duty. OH! I forgot - - -I usually down my Norwegian cup of ambient coffee that was sitting on my bed stand within reach. And by now I've had a wiener-dog sandwich smothered with mayonnaise.

This next thing was not in the normal order of the day, not in any normal day in Nord-a-koda, thanks to my buddy whom I'll call eyeballs just for old-time sake and for good reason. Anyway, eyeballs already had a date, guess he thought I needed some company so he set me up with a blind date.

And blind she was. She was literally blind- -only in one eye thank goodness, but blind as a bat in that eye. Her eye even looked bad. I felt bad for her that she couldn't get resources to fix that goofy looking eye, at least a little bit. Anyway I never forgot that night with that girl's eye. I gave him the nickname "eyeballs" and how fitting it was so I guess he figured the prank was fitting. I guess he wanted to have some fun but why me? I didn't ask her what had happened to her eye and she didn't say but I suspect she may have ran into a tree branch or something or scratched it too much with her long finger nails. She had long curly nails like a vampire. I wouldn't dare get out of bounds with her if I would of wanted to. Now don't laugh about the tree branch cause that did happen to a friend of mine who I'll simply call Ted. No, it wasn't Ted Williams.

I never fell for that trick again, ever. *And buddy if you are out there somewhere reading this, I hope you get a blind date some day. That'l learn ya'.*

This was the same buddy that knew the Home Economics Room window was unlocked in the high school where we, yes we, crawled in though the window and devowed orange soda pop til it came out our ears and a bunch of other goodies that was intended to be for the teachers next day meeting of the minds in the flooded gym. OH Yeah, the gym was flooded like I never ever saw a gym flooded like that before. There just happened to be a couple inches of water on the gym floor - - I mean it was a real flood. I can't imagine neither of us doing anything like that and leaving the fire hose hanging down from the balcony, still there the next morning. Beyond my better judgement, I came to school the next day so it wouldn't look obvious that I was in on that trick.

A meeting of the high-fluting minds on the gym floor that next morning caused some question why the floor was flooded. The school band played there on the floor earlier that morning and nobody said anything about the flood. I normally played in the band but I skipped out that morning which made some teachers question me the next day. Anyway they finally got over it.

KIDS, DON'T TRY THIS AT HOME or IN TOWN
cause the local police have billy clubs now. The town constable back then didn't a club, he didn't have anything like that. Remember the town population was about 300 and 100 of them was dogs.

WHAT TO WEAR TODAY
Sometimes when I am getting ready to go to town my better half will ask me "what are you going to wear"? I usually reply "shirt, socks, shorts, pants". That'l learn 'er.

GUARD RAILS AGAIN?
And now there are new guard rails replacing the ones that jumped out in front of me after that party, that's the Christmas party the night before the morning after. Oh, Yah. They made the road much wider too. Perhaps they hope I won't be able to clobber both rails so easy again if I have a couple Elmer Fudpucker drinks. These new rails look better and harder to bend than the old ones that nearly mangled me to death. Keep in mind, this all happened before 8 o'clock and I'm not responsible for my actions before that time.

Some things don't mix well. Wifie and I decided to go on vacation one time. She wanted to go to Ireland and rightfully so. I wanted to go to England so we compromised and went to Colorado. Lucky we had a friends place to stay that was within crawling distance from the local Moose Lodge club. No, we weren't hunting moose, we were indulging. Indulging in our favorite drinks, I mean Carol's favorite drinks like they were the last remaining drinks on earth. Anyway we, yes we, proceeds to have 1-2-3- and now I can't count anymore, drinks. Anyway somebody I know but ain't telling who, and is dear to my heart called Ralph on the water meter out back at least once to my knowledge. Of course by now my knowledge could be disputable. Anyway I slept for nearly 2 days and still had a scruciating head acke and felt like a zombie. Our dear friend Carol, bless her heart, commented "oh yeah, I forgot to tell you that altitude and booze don't mix".

CHAPTER 45

SATURDAY NIGHT ON THE FARM

A Tarzan movie in town or the Grand Ole Opry on the battery operated radio was our Saturday night excitement. And Ma had a hard time keeping up making her scrumptious homemade bread in the old cast iron cook stove. We, yes we kids and Dad would eat Ma's hot home made bread and milk (yes cow's milk not store milk) while listening to the Saturday night Grand Ole' Opry. When the radio battery went dead I got highly p_ _ _ _ _ cause I just loved Minnie Pearl. She's gone now too.

When the radio battery went caput us kids found other things to do like wheeling old car used car tires around the yard or in the pasture or in the woods. We had a set of old wheels thing that didn't know what it was so we called it "the thing". We would go ride the horse or the milk cows or the bull. The bull did n't like to be riden and he didn't like it that we rode his girl friend cows so he chased me one time and I didn't make it all the way over the barb wire fence. My bottom sorta' caught on the barbs and I still got marks on my bottom end to prove it.

Well I'm not old enough to remember when a shave and a haircut cost 2 bits but I do remember when just haircut was $ 3.00. Of course when I was a kid (1year to 15 years) Dad cut my hair. Sometimes he put a bowl over my head and kinda' went around the bowl very neatly. That got attention cause I combed my hair straight back like the old timers did. I still comb it pretty much straight back but I put a high wave in front and "some people's kids" call me Mountain top. Corky, if you are reading this—you just keep laughing.

I'm trying to have my barber, my hair-doer, my hair-fixer upper, my beauty restorer to give me a half a haircut but I get weird looks from her. Getting back to finding a beauty restorer, that's what I need today. Even a half restoration would do wonders for me.

CHAPTER 46

BEER IN THE DIAPER BAG

Or was it my size 5x coffee cup?

My other half and I had an episode and a conversation with Mr. Policeman one morning, after the night before, and we weren't talking about the weather:

Me: "No osifer, I mean officer we don't have any beer in the car".

Officer: "What's in that bag"?

Me: "That's my diaper bag. I mean my baby's diaper bag".

Officer: "What baby"?

Me: "Oh I just dropped him at the sitter".

Officer: "You dropped your baby? Where is it now? Let me see in that bag".

Me: "No, but Ok osifer, I mean officer. I wonder who put that in there"?

So I finally let him open it and look in. He dug in through the well used, ishy diapers and discovered a beer in the bottom. I had a hard time convincing him that the doctor said a beer a day was good for the baby's health. Anyway his hands were all dirty, juicy, sticky and messy by now so he said the heck with that and he let me go. That'l learn 'em.

Me: "Thank you osifer.

CHAPTER 47

QUIPS AND QUOTES

I don't booze no more, no more and no less. I never did much except one time for a couple years when I was in the Army.
I think it was a good thing that I was on guard duty a lot. Sometimes it was 3 to 4 nights a week. That only left 3 nights to drink-up. Good thing because Charlie, (the guy that bet me I would go back home on a ship when my 16 month tour was over) and I would make bed check at 10 o'clock PM ok but then after the osifer, I mean officer of the day came through the barricks he wouldn't check our boots under the bed . It was a good thing he didn't cause we (yes we) usually had a couple opened stale bottles of good ole 14% alcohol beer in our boots. By morning the stale warm beer would either kill us or cure us. We had more than one of those morning appetizers and survived them all.

I still haven't heard from Charlie since that last night in Korea when we got all boozed up, 3 sheets to the wind, he looked white as a sheet and I sprained my ankle, like you won't believe. That was the Charlie that helped carry me to the Medic that night.

Anyway, that banged up ankle kept from going home on the ship. I won that bet and Charlie if you are out there reading this book, remember ------------I told you so.

And Charlie, how is your blood pressure today? Mine was up, then down, then back up. It was up between 160 and 170 when the female nurse took it. I said to the man doctor "Funny thing", Why is that"?

So when the man Doctor took it and it was 125 and Doc said "I don't understand why".

I said "because she is a lot better looking than you are".

My pressure went up again when somebody's kid screwed around on the road in the middle of the night with the car lights turned off and I was stopped by Mr. Policeman again. We didn't talk about the weather cuz he wasn't in the mood so our conversation went something like this:

Me: "osifer, I mean Officer, why are you giving me a ticket"?

Officer: "you were speeding with your car lights turned off, why were you speeding"?

Me: "Well I had to blow the snow off my car".

Officer: why did you have the lights off?

Me: "well I can see the road just as good with them off cuz stuff is kinda' blurry anyway".

Officer: "what is that wet stuff on your pants and car seat"?

Me: "some cars don't have a good level dash on them to set a Norwegian coffee cup on it and it flipped upside down when I slammed on my brakes".

Officer: "why did you slam on your brakes"?

Me: "well I didn't want to tell you that I didn't see that stop sign back there so I wouldn't have to tell you "I'll stop twice at the next sign I see, oscifer I mean officer".

Officer: "well you take it easy now and slow down a little bit, I got to go now, I'm late for coffee".

A SHOCKING EXPERIENCE

The most shocking episode I ever had was when I was in a restroom in a Nuke plant down south. I was standing there facing the wall thing, doing my thing, relieving myself. Afterall, this was the place to do it when suddenly a lady walked in on me like she owned the place. I think my mouth dropped half way to the floor. She wasn't bothered any cause she knew the restroom was unisex. I didn't know that it was. She was a cleaning lady janitor. She cleaned the floors, the walls, the sinks, the stools, she cleaned the floors again, she cleaned the sinks again, she cleaned the walls again. I came to the final conclusion that she loved her job. I didn't know it was unisex or didn't see any sign in reference to that. It was the only restroom in the plant so I didn't have any choice anyway. Grafitei on the wall read "Please wash your hands before returning to the restaurant. It could help from spreading the HIVes".

HAPPY HUNTING

And now the moose have come to Northern Minnesota. The black bears have worked their way south as far as the Twin Cities. The wild turkeys are here picking bugs in my front yard and I love it.

Blacksmith Dick called me one night and he said "hey, some of us guys need another person to sign up for a moose license drawing and we want you to think about it. We need your luck to win the drawing".Well I said, "I have a long lost uncle in the DNR and maybe he can help". So I said "how much time do I have to say yes? Yes." About two weeks later an amazing thing came in the mail. It was the moose hunting permit. I couldn't wait to call "blacksmith Dick" any more than he couldn't wait to call me. He asked who was that guy in the DNR you know so well. "Oh, I just said that for the heck of it".

Anyway we went moose hunting. Can you imagine 5 of us guys climbing into an old beat up school bus on a morning after the night before, half snockered up before we got started? Shultsey as we called him, was our designated driver. I don't know who nominated him as designated driver but that was a mistake. A good time was had by all, all the way up to the camp site, including Shultsey the driver. I don't pray much but I was about ready to on that trip.

CHAPTER 48

THINGS GOT BETTER AGAIN

In the 1940's Ma always said "things will get better someday". And today things got better. Today we elected and inaugurated a new president and I believe that history will not repeat itself. But remember I don't want to touch politics even with an 11 foot pole.

Back then Ma made a lot of our cloths from used feed sacks and flour sacks. She wore out more than one sewing machine. She made cloths for my sister but knew well that I wouldn't wear a feed sack on my body.

And now the young people buy top notch pants and some wear them down to their crack. Oh well—that's the style I guess.

Pie crust decorating was the "in thing" in the olden days. The neighbor gal used a fork to mark the edges and make a design on the crust before baking it. Norway Grandma rolled her knuckles over the edges to make her mark. Ma used her right-hand thumb and put her thumb prints around the edges of the crust. And some peoples kids just smashed the edge with a butter knife.

We entertained our selves with whatever was available and reasonable. Jump rope was common as we would jump rope all the way to school. (wish I had some of that energy today). I remember rolling a worn out car tire around the yard, up and down the road, through the woods. We would ride one of the cows or the bull cow if the horses were at work. Dad had only one bull on the farm and he was a good one. He took care of all the cows ok.

Dad had an old dilapidated horse-drawn plow that he did the field work with for several years. Old "Flossy horse" pulled that plow by herself on a good day. On a bad day she could barely walk. I guess she had arthuritis or something. And finally her good days came to an end when she was 17 years old. The old plow has seen it's better days too.

Things got so much better that some close friends of ours got married and some peoples kids rigged up a hay rack with a wire fence on all sides and across the top with a lock on the door. We blindfolded the bride and groom and somehow got them to trust us and led them into the hayrack thing and locked the door. We pulled the rack, with them in it, down town to one of our favorite watering holes and said "see yous later". After a couple or so highballs (Harvey Wallbangers I think, if my memory serves me right,(that's kinda' scary) there was holloring and more holloring outside like you wouldn't believe. Here it was those two newly weds out in the rack, about 95 degrees in the shade, but no shade, sweating their whatever off. The bride said " I gotta' go to the bathroom". I said "ok there is the toilet in the rack sort'a behind those bales of straw". This was all sitting on main street, the main state highway so I don't know if she used that toilet but we didn't unlock the door. We went inside for another Harveywallbanger.

CHAPTER 49

THESE GOLDEN YEARS

No matter what people say, auctions keep you young by keeping the adrenalin flowing double time. Now at 73 I have carpenter's tunnel in my hands.

When I get out of bed in the morning, or in the middle of the night I slide slowly, gently, part way out on the edge of the bed, then slowly plant both feet on the floor to check for any feeling in them before I wobble to the bathroom.

I'm still on the green side of the grass. I'm not ready to let any grass grow under my feet or under my car tires. Some people's kids still call me lead foot when I put the pedal to the metal even if I don't have that 352 Police Interceptor Ford.

And these golden years bring us the latest fashions in cloths—boys and girls jeans with holes in them priced at $40 USD. Heck, I have some like that. I wonder of the "Needless Markup" stores would buy them from me? That's what my other half calls them and she won't shop there. Oh boy!

I like the narrow pants holder-uppers cause the wide ones make me sweat wider but we can't find them at that store.

You know they (who are they?) could keep the cost of overall jeans down if they wouldn't make them so long on the legs. I need to cut about 6" off of a 32" pant leg. That's crazy, just a couple months ago my inseam was 28", that was up my right leg on a good day.

Our latest addition to the family is a little guy 2 ½ years old and going on 6, if he'll make it without getting beat to death. He goes to the pot by himself but likes to write on the bathroom walls with his fingers after wiping his behind. Keeping in mind that he had poo-poo all over his hands, he did a real artistic presentation on Grandma's wall paper. That must be the Czechoslovakia part in him or maybe he is trying to do Norwegian rosemaling?

Remember those guard rails that jumped out in front of me one Friday evening years ago after chugging down a few hot toddies to get primed up for a Christmas party? Well, they have made that highway much wider since then and made those guard rails longer and stronger than they were when I drove on top of them. That's a change for the better in case I go partying again.

Well yes I missed that party but there were others of equal quality. Others put on by the best of friends, Porky, Blacksmith Dick, Senator, WI. Ray, The Buck, Colorado Ronney, Boomer, Johny, Hard Rock, Soft Rock, Welder Andy, our bus driver to the north woods moose hunt-- Shultsey, and the one and only "Painter".

CHAPTER 50

DOES HISTORY REPEAT?

And now I sit here all broken-hearted and I started thinking about what Dad had told me (and I know that's kinda' scary). He told me that before my time there was a big war, they called it World War I. Then there was a Great Depression, then the Dust Bowl, then another big war, they called it World War II.

The economy is going hay-wire again. Businesses are going belly-up including the well know retailer Montgomery Wards just to name a few. Unemployment lines are getting longer. Banks have been closing across the country and around the world. There is talk that the government may halt the production of the new gold-cladded coins.

And now in 2009 they had a second consecutive year of drought in Texas. The rainfall is 17 inches below the 2008 rain and 11 inches below normal. We need another Dust Bowl like we need a hole in the head.

Rig-amortis is setting into the stock market. The market acts like a yo-yo on a rubber string. I call it like I see it, a "slow pace'. I have a slow pace too but I know the reason why. I'm not sure about the stock market.

It seems like we feed half the world. It seems like we fight the other half. We don't need another big War.

They say that history repeats itself. I hope it don't.

I remember the aftermath of that "First Great Depression". I sincerely hope that we, The United States of America won't experience another one but it isn't looking real good.

Anyway time goes on, and as time goes on, our own family has multiplied to include 4 rug rats, their 5 rug rats, and one, and now two of their rug rats (great-grand rug rats). I don't think there will be anymore.

Remember that some people's kids did the craziest things? I was fortunate to be one of those kids that had kids, that had kids. That made me the Great Grandpa.

Our little great grand rug rat child grabs my pinky finger just like his Mommy, our Princess Queen did the hour she was born. My great grandson calls me Gr-r-r gampa. Golly he was only 2 then.

Looking at the brighter side--Strawberry and rhubarb pie is still my favorite.

And Ma and Dad are resting in peace up on the hill where eagles sore.

I hope you enjoyed this book, at least a little bit. There is one request I ask. If you liked the book, tell your friends, if you didn't like it, don't tell your friends.

And before we part there is one thing I ask of the man above— "Dear God, I hope we don't have a Second Great Depression".

Have a great day.

THE END.